SET ABLAZE

SET ABLAZE

Fanning the Flame of Your Soul and Service

An Expository Study of 2 Timothy

J. R. Raines

Set Ablaze: Fanning the Flame of Your Soul and Service
An Expository Study of 2 Timothy
Copyright © 2022 by J. R. Raines

Unless otherwise indicated, Scripture quotations are taken from the Holy Bible, English Standard Version, ESV® Text Edition: 2016, copyright © 2001 by Crossway Bibles, a publishing ministry of Good News Publishers. Used by permission. All rights reserved. www.crossway.org

Scripture quotations marked "BSB" are taken from The Holy Bible, Berean Study Bible, BSB. Copyright ©2016, 2018 by Bible Hub. Used by Permission. All Rights Reserved Worldwide. www.berean.bible

Scripture quotations marked "CEV" are from the Contemporary English Version. Copyright © 1991, 1992, 1995 by American Bible Society, Used by Permission. www.americanbible.org

Scripture quotations marked HCSB, are taken from the Holman Christian Standard Bible®. Copyright © 1999, 2000, 2002, 2003, 2009 by Holman Bible Publishers. Used by permission. HCSB is a federally registered trademark of Holman Bible Publishers.

Scripture quotations marked "MSG" are taken from The Message. Copyright 1993, 1994, 1995, 1996, 2000, 2001, 2002. Used by permission of NavPress Publishing Group. www.navpress.com

Scripture quotations marked "NIV" are taken from the Holy Bible, New International Version®, NIV®. Copyright © 1973, 1978, 1984 by Biblica, Inc.™ Used by permission of Zondervan. All rights reserved worldwide. www.zondervan.com

Set Ablaze Productions
raines.setablaze@gmail.com

Set Ablaze Productions

ISBN 978-0-578-35129-2

Book and E-book designed and formatted by EBook Listing Services
www.ebooklistingservices.com

Cover designed by Lester S. Ocampo ("Zealous")
www.99designs.com

ACKNOWLEDGMENTS

My Wife – In deep gratitude and appreciation to my lovely bride, who bore with my long absences during the writing of this book and whose encouragement and input gave me the support I needed at critical points of this journey.

Jeanette Windle – With appreciation to my editor for her patience and coaching as she helped me take a pretty rough document and turn it into a book. Her knowledge of the Scriptures and understanding of God's worldwide church were invaluable to this process.

TABLE OF CONTENTS

Introduction

Section I: Faith of Our Fathers

Section II: Keeping Ablaze Your Holy Spirit Gifts

Section III: Gifts from Our Father

Section IV: Cultivating the Right Mindset

Section V: Suffering for the Gospel

Section VI: A Vessel for God's Service

BOOK CONTENT

SECTIONS: This book is divided into topical sections according to the order its themes appear in 2 Timothy. The chapter topics as well are ordered sequentially to the life of a disciple.

SUGGESTED PRAYERS: Each section has a suggested historic prayer at the beginning to focus on while reading that section. The intent is to help center your heart on that particular topic as well as invite God to do a work in your soul and service related to that topic. In choosing the various prayers, I have tried to represent a broad spectrum of different time periods and branches of the Christian church.

SELECTED PASSAGES: Each chapter focuses on a specific scriptural passage within 2 Timothy from which the chapter's main theme is taken. I have tried to stay true thematically and chronologically to how Paul structured this epistle. Some chapters also include supporting texts from epistles of Paul, especially Paul's first letter to Timothy, the book of Acts, or occasional other Old and New Testament supplementary passages. These texts are intended to give fuller depth to the topics Paul covers in 2 Timothy.

GOING DEEPER: At the end of each section, you will find suggested activities to help you engage more deeply with the material of that section. I would encourage you to participate in these activities as they were created to help you own and apply the spiritual truths found in the previous chapters.

MENTOR: I am convinced that the impact of this book will be maximized when used as a tool within a mentor/mentee relationship, much as was the apostle Paul's original intent in writing this epistle to Timothy. If this is not possible, the material covered will still be greatly profitable for personal study as well as large-group training settings.

KEY TERMS: It is important to understand that when the terms *church* and *ministry* are used in this book, church is not referring to a building but people, and ministry is not referring to a paid position but a lifestyle of service to God.

In dedication to Jesus Christ, my savior and friend. May your kingdom come on earth as it is in heaven.

INTRODUCTION

To me whom am but black, cold charcoal, grant, O Lord, that by the fire of Pentecost, I may be set ablaze.

—Prayer from St. John of Damascus
Syrian monk, A.D. 675 – 749

When I stood up from my seat, there was no way I could have fully understood how that simple action would set the trajectory for the rest of my life. I was a young teen attending our denomination's summer camp meetings when the Holy Spirit gripped me with a challenge I'd never heard to that point in my life and have never heard since. It went something like this:

"Normally, people ask you to consider serving God in overseas mission work. But I would like to switch that up and ask you to make a commitment towards cross-cultural mission work for the rest of your life unless God closes every door in this endeavor."

This challenge came from my youth pastor, who was himself heading off to serve God in Tanzania, East Africa. Looking back, it's difficult to explain everything that was going on inside me at that moment. All I can say is that God showed up, so I stood up to symbolize my commitment to him. There have been times when I have wavered and lost focus, but God always brought me back to that vow I made to him when I stood up from my seat.

So who am I? Foremost, I am a child of God. Beyond that, I'd say the single most important thing that has defined me to this point in my life has been a call to mission work. This call has taken me all over the world. I've had the privilege of serving God for extended periods in several locations, including two years on an Indian Ocean island, ten years in East Africa, and two years in the Middle East. For the security of those still serving in some of these settings, I will for the most part not be mentioning specific locations.

The anecdotes I share in this book aren't always in chronological order. So let me first give some background information and general outline of major life events to provide context.

After living abroad for most of my adult life, I have a hard time saying where "home" is. But my passport tells me I'm a citizen of the United States. I was born and raised in southeastern Pennsylvania, an area known as Pennsylvania Dutch country due to its high population of German Amish and Mennonites (for non-locals, Pennsylvania Dutch refers to German ethnicity, not Dutch). My own ethnic heritage is German Mennonite.

While I never forgot that commitment I made in my early teens to serve God in overseas mission work, there were times throughout high school and even into Bible College when I wasn't living a focused life towards this end. I am so grateful for God's persistence and interventions that brought me to a point of total surrender midway through college.

After graduating from college, I spent a period serving my home church. I was then sent to be trained in a two-year mission program located in the Indian Ocean. From there I came back to the United States, where I taught Bible and social studies in a Christian school for four years. After this, I returned overseas to serve ten years in East Africa as part of an Unreached People project (i.e., people groups with less than two percent Christian population).

During a stint stateside while serving in East Africa, I met my wonderful and incredibly gifted wife. After we were married, she joined me in my calling. When our work in East Africa was finished, we followed God's call to the 10/40 Window, a section of the planet from ten to forty degrees north of the equator in which falls the largest percentage of the planet's poverty and political upheaval as well as the least access to the gospel of Jesus Christ.

Fallout from the COVID-19 pandemic led to moving back to the United States in 2020. While my wife and I dearly miss the wonderful friends we've left behind overseas, we also know God uses all kinds of situations to lead us on "right paths, for his name's sake (Psalm 23:3)."

I wrote the lion's share of the following manuscript during this pandemic when I could not do "ministry as usual." Much of its content had been percolating in my mind and heart for several years. Living in social isolation for months on end finally allowed me the space to get it down on paper. A dear friend and prayer partner gave me the final push I needed when he told me, "We may never get a time like this again in our lives. Whatever you have been desiring to do but could not, this is the time."

For me, that was documenting a journey of change and renewal. I am now in my mid-forties, and it seems everything in my life is changing. My career. My country of residence. My body. I am noticing other changes as well. Many influential people I admire and have matured under in ministry are reaching retirement age and starting to transition out of their leadership positions. This observation has brought home the reality that it will soon be my generation's turn to step into their leadership void.

I am deeply concerned about this because I sense that, even as the influence of my generation of leadership increases, our personal and spiritual fires are in danger of growing cold. This is a dilemma and struggle that no doubt has faced emerging spiritual leaders of every age, gender, and culture. Stepping into leadership gaps only magnifies the clear need for tending their own fires.

Nor is this dilemma unique to the twenty-first century. Timothy, a youthful disciple of the apostle Paul, was facing a very similar situation when he received a letter from his mentor and spiritual father that we know today as "The Second Epistle of Paul to Timothy" or more commonly as 2 Timothy.

Paul wrote this particular letter to Timothy as a guide to help him through a pivotal time in his ministry. It is a moment every Christian in any type of ministry faces when we have to decide, whether for the first or fortieth time, to either hang it all up or step into all that God has for us. Paul encouraged Timothy through this critical juncture by fanning the fires of his faith and ministry.

Over the following chapters, we will be taking a close look at Paul's letter to Timothy and how it applies to today's Christian ministry leader in whatever unique service to which God has called them. My aim in writing this book is the same as Paul's for Timothy. I pray that God will use these chapters to set ablaze your own faith and ministry during pivotal times in your life. I also pray that it will act as a guide to help you transition into a new period of powerful service for our Lord and Savior.

SECTION ONE:
FAITH OF OUR FATHERS

Blessed are you, O Lord our God and God of our fathers, the God of Abraham, the God of Isaac, and the God of Jacob, the great, mighty, and revered God, the Most High God who bestows loving kindnesses, the creator of all things, who remembers the good deeds of the patriarchs and in love will bring a redeemer to their children's children for his name's sake. O king, helper, savior, and shield. Blessed are you, O Lord, the shield of Abraham.

—Portion from *The Standing Prayer*
Jewish Liturgy, 4th century B.C.

CHAPTER ONE
SERVING THE GOD OF OUR FATHERS

Paul, an apostle of Christ Jesus by the will of God according to the promise of the life that is in Christ Jesus, to Timothy, my beloved child: Grace, mercy, and peace from God the Father and Christ Jesus our Lord. I thank God whom I serve, as did my ancestors, with a clear conscience, as I remember you constantly in my prayers night and day.

—2 Timothy 1:1-3

. . . circumcised on the eighth day of the people of Israel, of the tribe of Benjamin, a Hebrew of Hebrews; as to the law, a Pharisee.

—Philippians 3:5

In the first century A.D., the city of Rome had over a million people living within its walls but only one prison. It was a dark, foul-smelling place reserved for high-profile prisoners on their way to execution. Any person unfortunate enough to be lowered into its dungeon could be quite certain they were not long for this world. That is why the apostle Paul wrote the following when he was imprisoned there.

> For I am already being poured out as a drink offering, and the time of my departure has come. I have fought the good fight, I have finished the race, I have kept the faith.
>
> —2 Timothy 4:6-7

Enemy of the State

The Roman historian Tacitus records that the apostle Paul was charged with the crime of "hatred against mankind." This was a weighty-sounding accusation commonly leveled against those who refused to worship the Roman pantheon of gods or make offerings to the current Roman emperor. If this accusation against Paul was confirmed to be true, then as an influential religious figure he would be considered a threat to the empire, therefore an enemy of the state. One thing Paul could count on with Rome was that it always dealt mercilessly with its enemies. Knowing he might never again see his co-minister Timothy, Paul pulled out a piece of parchment and wrote him a farewell letter. This letter as well as Paul's other epistles were recognized as divinely inspired by the early church, including the apostle Peter himself (2 Peter 3:16), and is found in our New Testament canon of Scripture.

SERVING THE GOD OF MY ANCESTORS

After Paul's initial greetings to Timothy, he begins the main body of his letter with this phrase: "I thank God whom I serve, as did my ancestors, with a clear conscience."

This opening statement may seem at first unpretentious. But it is quite powerful when we recall the circumstances in which Paul wrote it. When we add to this Paul's later reference to being a "drink offering" to his God (4:6), i.e., that his blood would be poured out at his impending execution, we are compelled to ask, "Who was the God of Paul's ancestors that he felt so grateful to serve even in the face of death?"

We find the answer to this question in Philippians 3:5, the second focus passage given at the beginning of this chapter, where Paul gives some biographical information about himself. Paul identified himself as a "Hebrew of the Hebrews." The name Hebrew originated from Abraham, who was identified as being of the Hebrew people (Genesis 14:13). So while the nation of Israel descended from Jacob's twelve sons and the tribes they would become, Abraham, Isaac, and Jacob were themselves descendants from a larger Mesopotamian people group called the Hebrews. Joshua 24:2 says that the Hebrews had a history of serving other gods, and it connects them to a geographical area known for idolatry and worship of the moon. It was out of this pagan background that Yahweh, the creator God of all things, called Abraham and his descendants to be his people, set apart to serve him alone.

ISRAEL'S DEAL WITH ROME

Like the original Hebrew people, it was commonplace for the nations of the Roman Empire to worship many gods. However, the Jewish people (at the time of Christ, the Israelites were more commonly known as the Jews) would define themselves by this period as worshipping the one and only God of their ancestors Abraham, Isaac, and Jacob. The Shema, the traditional morning and evening prayer from the final discourse of Moses to the people of Israel, had become the cry of their monotheistic hearts.

> Hear, O Israel: **The Lord our God, the Lord is one.** You shall love the Lord your God with all your heart and with all your soul and with all your might. (emphasis mine)
>
> —Deuteronomy 6:4-5

This is why Rome decided against trying to force their pantheon of gods on the Jewish people when they took control of Israel in 63 B.C. They knew it would be a losing battle, so instead they opted for a more shrewd approach by making a deal with Israel. This deal allowed the Jews some local religious authority that included freedom to sacrifice to the God of their ancestors instead of to the emperor. In return for these religious privileges, which were monitored and could be revoked, they had to agree to submit to Roman rule.

As a "Hebrew of Hebrews" living under this deal, Paul should have been free to worship the God of his ancestors without worry.

Why then was he writing this letter to Timothy in a dank Roman dungeon while awaiting trial and execution as an enemy of the state? The official answer according to Nero, an infamously cruel Roman emperor, was that Paul was part of a fanatical and destructive religious sect called Christians. But the real reason for singling Paul out for persecution was that, while he indeed worshipped the God of his ancestors, Paul's beliefs about God were fundamentally different from the Jewish religious establishment, whom Rome could manage through their deal. The message Paul was preaching was about a new kingdom, one that could not be compromised and therefore controlled. This was something neither the Jewish religious leaders nor the Roman Empire could tolerate.

A DANGEROUS MESSAGE OF HOPE FOR ALL NATIONS

By the time of Paul, the religious rulers of Israel, which included a party known as the Pharisees, had turned the "faith of their fathers" into the laws and bylaws of their fathers. We've already seen in Paul's biography above that he identified as a member of this works-oriented sect. In fact, other Scripture passages indicate he grew up and studied under the Pharisees (Acts 22:2-5). But after he met Christ, Paul stated:

Indeed, I count everything as loss because of the surpassing worth of knowing Christ Jesus my Lord. For his sake I have suffered the loss of all things and count them as rubbish, in order that I may gain Christ and be found in him, not having a righteousness of my own that comes from the law, but that which comes through faith in Christ, the righteousness from God that depends on faith.

— Philippians 3:8-9

The idea that salvation could be obtained only through faith in Christ was in direct opposition to everything the Jewish religious establishment espoused. Most of them saw it as a false teaching being spread by a heretic. In contrast, Paul made clear that he wasn't making up a new religion. Rather, he was teaching a faith that had always existed but only now through Jesus Christ could be fully understood, as Paul laid out in his letter to Timothy.

> Who [God] saved us and called us to a holy calling, not because of our works but because of his own purpose and grace, which **he gave us in Christ Jesus before the ages began, and which now has been manifested through the appearing of our Savior Christ Jesus**, who abolished death and brought life and immortality to light through the gospel. (emphasis mine)
>
> —2 Timothy 1:9-10

To build his case, Paul went back to the covenant God made with Abraham, Isaac, and Jacob that God would bless the nations of the world through their descendants, as we see in the epistle Paul wrote to the Roman Christians some years before his imprisonment in Rome.

> **For the promise to Abraham . . . did not come through the law but through the righteousness of faith** . . . in order that the promise may rest

on grace and be guaranteed to all his offspring—not only to the adherent of the law but **also to the one who shares the faith of Abraham, who is the father of us all,** as it is written, "I have made you the father of many nations . . . That is why his faith was "counted to him as righteousness." But the words "it was counted to him" **were not written for his sake alone, but for ours also. It will be counted to us who believe in him who raised from the dead Jesus our Lord,** who was delivered up for our trespasses and raised for our justification. (emphasis mine)

—Romans 4:13-25

What Paul is saying here is that Abraham did nothing to earn this covenant with God. Abraham received both the covenant and the righteousness of God through his faith in God's works rather than through his own work. Of additional significance in this letter to the Romans is that the message of righteousness through faith was not unique to Abraham but for all "who believe in him who raised from the dead Jesus our Lord" (4:25).

The ramifications of Paul's message were immense because it broke down the political walls between Roman and Jewish citizens. Since Abraham was a model of faith in God, all who put their trust in God could consider Abraham their spiritual father. All were equally invited to join Jesus in his kingdom, something infinitely greater than the glory of Rome or the "laws of our fathers" that the Jewish religious establishment had made the center of their religion.

This was a dangerous ideology to those who desired to hold on to their physical kingdoms at all cost. Rome knew this new Christian sect had the power to turn into a movement that could collapse established religions and long-held empires. For them as for the Jewish leaders, there was only one answer. Christianity needed to be snuffed out along with all those who proclaimed it. That is how Paul, a Hebrew of Hebrews, found himself in a Roman dungeon grateful to be serving the God of his ancestors to the very end. Even in the face of death, he was at peace, knowing that Rome could kill his body but could not stop God's kingdom.

REFLECT AND APPLY

Paul had the choice of serving the political establishment, the man-made religious establishment, or the true God of Abraham, Isaac, and Jacob. Take a moment and think about where your time is spent and your hope is placed. What does that tell you about who you are serving?

CHAPTER TWO
SORTING THROUGH OUR FAITH LEGACIES

As I remember your tears, I long to see you that I may be filled with joy. I am reminded of your sincere faith, a faith that dwelt first in your grandmother Lois and your mother Eunice and now, I am sure, dwells in you as well.

—2 Timothy 1:4-5

ALL GENUINE DISCIPLES OF CHRIST ARE SO in part because of the faithful witness of those who came before them. Jesus told his twelve apostles to go into all the world and make disciples (Matthew 28:16-20). This command is often called the Great Commission. Because these twelve men and every following generation of disciples chose to obey this command, we who are Christians today have had the privilege of hearing the good news of Christ and becoming his disciples as well. This chain of disciple-makers is our faith legacy.

OF SINNERS AND SAINTS

When we first come to Christ, the men and women who make up our personal faith legacy often seem larger than life. As we grow older, mature in our own faith, and spend more time in real community with these people of whom we think so highly, they start to take on flesh and blood. As we witness them living imperfect lives, we begin to notice the scars and blemishes that come with real skin. We are shocked when we finally see them as they actually are, flawed and very human.

At this moment of disillusionment, it is not unusual to be haunted with the thought: "If they aren't all I thought them to be, maybe the message of faith they brought me isn't either."

In an effort to make sense of this quandary, we may be tempted to reject the messenger as well as their message. While this is a natural reaction, it doesn't take into account the apostle Paul's reminder in the first letter we have from Paul to his son in the faith, Timothy.

> Christ Jesus came into the world to save sinners, of whom I am the foremost.
>
> —1 Timothy 1:15

The reality has always been that the Christians ahead of us in the faith, whom we respect and hold to be saints, are also sinners who have been saved by grace just like us. It is also important to remember that the process of becoming Christ-like disciples is a lifelong journey filled with spiritual mountains, valleys, and plateaus. The apostle Paul reminded the Corinthian church that we are all "being transformed" into Christ's image (2 Corinthians 3:18). He also encouraged the Philippian church:

> And I am sure of this, that **he who began a good work in you will bring it to completion** at the day of Jesus Christ. (emphasis mine)
>
> —Philippians 1:6

God's saints who are still living on this earth just aren't complete yet. Rather, they are a good work in progress that will indeed be complete once we are in the presence of our Savior. On any given day, a disciple of Christ may act like the sinner they were, the saint they are, or someone transitioning between the two. So be patient and give them the same grace you want others to give you.

VERY HUMAN FAITH LEGACIES

I've often had to work through these truths myself as I come from a sincere but very human faith legacy. My grandfather dedicated his life to running a small inner-city church. To the best of my knowledge, his faith was genuine. But there was another side to him that appeared in the stories my dad would occasionally tell his own children. This side of my grandfather was full of brokenness and anger, which often spilled out on his family at home.

Exodus 34:7 speaks of how "the iniquity of the fathers" can be visited upon "the children and the children's children to the third and the fourth generation." In other words, the sins of one or both parents can affect the lives of their children and children's children. An example would be how growing up in a broken, angry home can foster angry adults who still struggle with the shame of their past. This is what we often term "generational family sins."

We need only look at the forefathers of the nation of Israel for examples. Abraham and Isaac both were responsible for their wives ending up in a king's harem when they lied to save their own necks (Genesis 12, 20, 26). That sin of deceit was passed down to Jacob, the schemer who plotted to steal his brother's birthright (Genesis 26-27). Finally, his own sons hatched a plan to deceive Jacob and sell their brother Joseph into slavery (Genesis 37). Every generation is responsible for their own life choices. But a father can model behaviors that will encourage healthy or destructive patterns for generations to come.

When I think of my own father, who is now with his Savior, I picture him with his Bible in hand surrounded by devotionals and commentaries.

Another image I have is him on his knees late at night in prayer. I can remember stopping by his study and having deep spiritual conversations with him, where we would share what God was teaching us in his Word.

My father's love for God and the Bible came from his own father. But with this wonderful heritage, he also inherited his father's anger. So when I remember my father, I also see scenes where his anger flared up in destructive ways. How do I reconcile the sincere faith of my grandfather and father with their broken and destructive sides? Does their brokenness negate their faith?

It is easy to make that connection between my father and grandfather. But what of Abraham, Isaac, and Jacob? What of myself? I love God with a sincere faith. I have walked with God most of my life. I have given myself to full-time cross-cultural ministry. I long to see the lost come to know Christ. Yet I am only now beginning to break free from the chains that have shackled me to the sins of my fathers. Like my grandfather and father, I also struggle with anger.

Part of that comes from destructive life patterns passed down to me. But part of that I just have to acknowledge as my own sin and selfishness. God has been healing me from this, but it is a slow, painful process, and I often go back to the very things from which God has freed me. For better or worse, we inherit so much from our parents. I am often tempted to focus on the worst, but I will be eternally grateful for my faith legacy, even though it is very messy and human.

TIMOTHY'S FAITH LEGACY

In 2 Timothy 1:4-5, we see that Timothy's family also had a faith legacy, which was strong in some ways and lacking in others. Timothy inherited his faith from his mother Eunice and his grandmother Lois, who had passed down to him their own sincere love for God. But where were the men in all this? Where was Timothy's dad? Where was his grandfather? Not named in this passage and not present on a spiritual level at least.

We are still asking the same questions in our families, churches, and ministries. Where are the men? Who is protecting and nurturing faith communities in the ways of God? If someone is doing this, it is often the mothers because the men are so wrapped up in their own brokenness they can't or won't step into their God-given role as spiritual leader of their home. Instead, they hide themselves in work or play.

We celebrate mothers who take a stand in their homes and commit to raising their children in the faith as followers of Jesus Christ. But we also mourn for families who long for their fathers and husbands to step up and shepherd their households the way Jesus shepherds his church, as commanded in Scripture (Ephesians 5:22-32, 6:1-3; Colossian 3:18-21; 1 Peter 5:2-4).

In his letters to Timothy, Paul addresses the issue of fear in Timothy's life and ministry. As I read these passages, I can't help wondering if the reason why Timothy seems so prone to fear is because his father was absent in his young life. Was he always away on business? Was he overly authoritative or emotionally distant?

God has not seen fit to allow us to peer into that window. But we know Timothy's father was an unbelieving Greek and a silent figure in Timothy's spiritual development (Acts 16:1). Thank God for Timothy's mother Eunice, who took over that crucial role in his childhood. Thank God also for Paul, who stepped into Timothy's life as a spiritual father. God is good like that, often bringing spiritual parents into our lives when our birth parents are unable or unwilling to be that for us.

Just as nothing is said about Timothy's father, we have no record of Paul having children or even being married. In fact, we know Paul was single during his missionary career at least (1 Corinthians 7:1-7, 9:5). So it was natural Paul and Timothy should become the father and son the other never had. Paul starts off his letter to Timothy by calling him his dearly loved son. That is not the language of an assigned mentor but of a special parental-child relationship. Paul took his role as Timothy's spiritual father seriously and invested his life into Timothy.

It is noteworthy that after Paul greets Timothy, the first thing he does is reminisce about Timothy's spiritual inheritance. He does this by mentioning the names of those in Timothy's life from whom he received his sincere faith. Paul does this for a reason. He is fanning the flame of Timothy's soul and ministry by anchoring them to a genuine faith legacy. He wants Timothy to look back, remember, and be encouraged that his faith heritage, which was certainly very human at times, was still sincere and very real.

REFLECT AND APPLY

Timothy's faith legacy included his mother, grandmother, and spiritual mentor Paul. Who has been a part of your faith legacy? Take time to identify and appreciate these servants of God who passed on to you their genuine love for the Lord.

CHAPTER THREE

CELEBRATING OUR FAITH HEROES

As I remember your tears, I long to see you that I may be filled with joy. I am reminded of your sincere faith, a faith that dwelt first in your grandmother Lois and your mother Eunice and now, I am sure, dwells in you as well.

—2 Timothy 1:4-5

By faith Abel offered to God a more acceptable sacrifice than Cain, through which he was commended as righteous, God commending him by accepting his gifts. And through his faith, though he died, he still speaks. By faith Enoch was taken up so that he should not see death, and he was not found, because God had taken him. Now before he was taken he was commended as having pleased God. And without faith it is impossible to please him, for whoever would draw near to God must believe that he exists and that he rewards those who seek him.

—Hebrews 11:4-6

HEBREWS CHAPTER ELEVEN IS OFTEN REFERENCED as the "roll call of faith" since the entire chapter gives a list from Abel, Enoch, Noah, Abraham, Jacob, Joseph, Moses, Samuel, David, the prophets, the martyrs, even Rahab the prostitute, all who followed God at great cost by faith. When I read of Timothy's faith legacy in 2 Timothy 1:4-5, my thoughts go to the eleventh chapter of Hebrews. Both of these passages call us to remember our faith legacies. We don't need to spit into a test tube and send it to a lab to get our spiritual ancestry report because Hebrew 11 has already provided us with a list of the great men and women of old who have given us their spiritual DNA.

The author of Hebrews starts with Abel, whose sacrifice of faith ultimately cost him his life. Though Abel is dead, his sacrifice still inspires us to give the best of what we have to God. The roll call moves on to Enoch, who walked with God. God loved their fellowship together so much that he took Enoch to heaven long before his natural life span was up (Genesis 3:23-24) to be with him on a more permanent basis. I imagine they are still enjoying their strolls along heaven's streets of gold.

The roll call of faith goes on and on, all the way up through the great persecution that preceded the reestablishment of Israel as a truly monotheistic people (google the Maccabees and Antiochus Epiphanes if you aren't familiar with that intertestamental period). We celebrate these great men and women of God because of the lives of faith they lived. And even if we are not genetically members of the Jewish people, we remember them as our spiritual ancestors, our spiritual tribe.

A GREAT CLOUD OF WITNESSES

The Hebrews 11 roll call of faith ends with the reminder that all those faithful spiritual ancestors died still looking forward in faith to the hope of a coming Savior (11:39-40). But that doesn't mean they didn't get to see the fulfillment of their faith. The very next verses found in Hebrews 12 tell us:

> Therefore, **since we are surrounded by so great a cloud of witnesses,** let us also lay aside every weight, and sin which clings so closely, and let us run with endurance the race that is set before us, looking to Jesus, the founder and perfecter of our faith, who for the joy that was set before him endured the cross, despising the shame, and is seated at the right hand of the throne of God. (emphasis mine)
>
> —Hebrews 12:1-2

In context, that "cloud of witnesses" is precisely the roll call of faith heroes listed in the previous chapter—and presumably every other faithful saint who didn't make the list. I used to picture them sitting on bleachers in the clouds or maybe in a super-stadium in heaven watching our lives on a jumbo screen.

If I'm honest, it can be unnerving to picture this large crowd of "faithful greats" getting a front-row seat to my life because I haven't always been proud of what they might see. I was grateful when I finally realized the image being given here isn't that these faith heroes are sitting up in heaven spying on our words and actions day and night. Instead, this large crowd of heroes, who've gone on before us into God's presence, witness to us through their lives and even deaths as to what true faith entails. To put it in other terms, they are not witnessing **us** but **to us**, so we in turn can follow their example and become faithful witnesses to those who come behind us.

Why is it so important that we commemorate a bunch of people long dead and gone? For the same reason every tribe and people group tell stories, sing songs, and put on plays about their folk heroes. The heroes on this roll call of faith are both larger than life and ordinary people like us with incredible stories that need to be told to each new generation. That is why God gives us their stories in the Bible as well as in Jewish and church history. Through the retelling of their deeds, they inspire us to keep alive the values and collective wisdom of our people.

Remembering and celebrating our faith heroes is a critical component in knowing who we are and what we stand for. Nonetheless, the roll call in Hebrews 11 was incomplete even as it was written. The author goes on to say:

> Time would fail me to tell of Gideon, Barak, Samson, Jephthah, of David and Samuel and the prophets—who through faith conquered kingdoms, enforced justice, obtained promises, stopped the mouths of lions, quenched the power of fire, escaped the edge of the sword . . . Others suffered mocking and flogging, and even chains and imprisonment. They were stoned, they were sawn in two, they were killed with the sword. They went about in skins of sheep and goats, destitute, afflicted, mistreated—of whom the world was not worthy.
>
> —Hebrews 11:32-38

If this list was incomplete when it was assembled two thousand years ago, can you imagine how long it would be if it was current to the present day? What other faith heroes might we be surprised to find on that list?

GET INSPIRED BY OUR FAITH HEROES

There is a long list of saints celebrated by much of Christendom. New Testament personages like the apostles, Stephen the first martyr, Joseph of Arimathea, Tabitha who was raised from the dead by the apostle Peter, and of course Mary the mother of Jesus. And later church heroes of faith like St. Augustine, St. Francis of Assisi, St. Patrick of Ireland, Joan of Arc, etc. In fact, more than ten thousand "venerated saints" have made the "roll call of faith" across the spectrum of the Christian church globally over the last two thousand years.

While we may be familiar with the most common names, there is also a "great cloud of witnesses" that we will often be blessed to encounter only if we are willing to step outside of our own church, preferred denomination, community, even country to explore the diversity that exists in Christ's universal church. I had the joy of being introduced to one of these inspiring faith heroes while on a trip to Egypt. If you are ever privileged to travel there, do yourself a favor and visit the Cave Church of the Zabbaleen, otherwise known as Saint Simon's Monastery, just outside of Cairo in the Mokattam Mountain.

That's right, *in* the mountain. The church is actually located in a massive cave that seats about twenty thousand people. And this is only one of several caves local Orthodox Christians use for their gatherings. While I was visiting a smaller cave, my guide showed me a mural of Saint Simon, the church's namesake, and told me his story.

Simon was a tenth-century shoemaker. One day while measuring the foot of a female customer, he glanced up and saw enough of her leg to fill him with desire. This led him to take literally the advice of Jesus in his Sermon on the Mount.

> But I say to you that everyone who looks at a woman with lustful intent has already committed adultery with her in his heart. **If your right eye causes you to sin, tear it out** and throw it away. For it is better that you lose one of your members than that your whole body be thrown into hell. (emphasis added)
>
> —Matthew 5:28-29

Simon sought to guard his soul by gauging out the offending eye with the leatherwork needle in his hand. That could have been the end of the story except that God honored Simon's faith by calling on the shoemaker to lead the church in Egypt through their own "Elijah on Mt. Carmel" (1 Kings 18:16-45) showdown.

This power encounter was instigated by the Fatimid Caliph Al-Muizz, ruler of Egypt at this time. The caliph hosted religious debates in his palace between the three main religions of his kingdom: Islam, Christianity, and Judaism. One day after a heated discussion, the caliph declared that if Christianity was true, the Egyptian Christians should be able to move a mountain just as Jesus had once said.

For truly, I say to you, if you have faith like a grain of mustard seed, you will say to this mountain, "Move from here to there," and it will move, and nothing will be impossible for you.

—Matthew 17:20

The caliph gave the Egyptian Christians three days to prepare for this miracle. If they failed, he would kill all the Christians within his territory. As the Egyptian believers prepared for this event, they realized they would indeed need to have the faith Jesus spoke of if they were to move a literal mountain. So they called on Simon, the shoemaker who had lived out his faith in such a simple but radical way.

When the appointed day came, the caliph and all his soldiers gathered at the chosen mountain to see what would happen. Simon instructed the Christians to pray three times: "God have mercy." As they recited this simple prayer in faith, the mountain shook as though a large earthquake had hit it. Then it rose in the air and moved. Seeing this, the caliph gave praise to God and admitted this miracle showed that the Christians' faith was true. After the crowd had settled down, they turned to find Simon, but he was no longer there.

This story inspires me for a lot of reasons. First, Simon is a simple guy just trying to live out his faith in radical ways. He is a shoemaker, not some renowned desert hermit or pope. I also love that God looks at our hearts and faith, not our titles or fancy prayers. When I hear this story, I get a stirring in the embers of my soul. My faith grows stronger as I think to myself, *Simon was a simple man just like me, but God used him to do something great for his kingdom.*

Like the folk heroes of old, Simon the shoemaker is at once larger than life and attainable as an ordinary human being just like us. I am honored to have him as part of my spiritual legacy. Simon is only one of a host of faith heroes in my life. Some of these people have encouraged me from the pages of church history. Others have physically stepped into my life for a time. But all of them have inspired me in my faith walk during critical moments.

There is Athanasius of Alexandria, who fought with courage against the heresies that threatened the existence of the early church. There is St. Patrick, who by faith escaped slavery, then made it his life's mission to evangelize his captors in Ireland. There is also Keith Green, contemporary Christian musician who died in a tragic small-plane accident at just twenty-eight years of age. His passion for God and prophetic voice exemplified in his music challenged the church to burn for Jesus and greatly impacted my own heart.

Then there are the faith heroes I've been privileged to have in my own personal life. My high school soccer coach Mr. Bergey, who pushed me beyond what I thought I was capable of and inspired me to excellence. My Christian Service Brigade captain Mr. Keiper, who entrusted me with leadership and showed me that real men can be godly. Pastor Jeff, who looked past my immaturity and impulsiveness and mentored me during a very formational chapter of my life. Page space doesn't allow me to talk about all the others who impacted my life at critical moments like Mark, Chris and Beka, Pastor Boone . . .

All the above aren't just dynamic figures from the pages of history or inspiring personalities who briefly walked across the stage of my own life.

They are people from my spiritual tribe, the people of God, and their DNA of faith runs deep in my blood. We are and will always be connected in Christ. Yes, many of these faith heroes have been broken, very human people. But in those moments when they stepped out in faith, they shook the world for Jesus. At least one literally moved a mountain in the process.

So as I reflect on their lives, I am reminded of how much all of us are capable of when we walk with God. I am filled with gratitude that through their faith I have been invited into something so much greater than myself. And I am inspired to join their ranks as a broken, very human man who by faith can engage this world for Jesus and in the process just might move a mountain.

REFLECT AND APPLY

Write down the list of your faith heroes, both living and dead. How have they stirred the embers of your soul at different junctures in your life?

Going Deeper

Suggested Activities

1. 1 Peter 3:15 says that we are to be ready at any moment to share about the hope we have in Christ. In Philippians 3, Paul gives his testimony, or story, of how he came to truly serve the God of Abraham, Isaac, and Jacob. Write out your own testimony using the structure that Paul used in this passage.

   - What did I put my confidence in before I met Christ?
   - How did coming to know (experience) Christ change that?
   - What does Christ mean to me now?
   - Communicate that you are not perfect but are striving to live like Christ.
   - Challenge others to follow Christ like you are.

2. Track down one of your faith heroes who is still alive and express to them in your preferred method of communication (i.e., personal visit, phone call, written letter, email, etc.) how they have impacted your life.

3. The universal church of Christ is currently divided into three main branches: Orthodox, Catholic, and Protestant. Choose a different branch than the one you are currently part of or grew up in and read a biography about one of their faith heroes.

SUGGESTED READING:

Heroes of the Faith by Gene Fedele.

SECTION TWO:
KEEPING ABLAZE YOUR HOLY SPIRIT GIFTS

Dear Lord Christ, give us your Holy Spirit and gifts, not for our own glory but for the service and edifying of all Christendom. This is the only reason you give your Spirit, as St. Paul says in 1 Corinthians 12, "You give to each one according to your will." That is, not for our shame or sin or vanity, but for your praise and glory and love and thanks for your inexpressible grace and gifts forever. Amen.

—Martin Luther
Reformation priest, sixteenth century

CHAPTER FOUR

RECOGNIZING GOD'S GIFTS WITHIN YOU

For this reason I remind you to fan into flame the gift of God, which is in you through the laying on of my hands.

—2 Timothy 1:6

Do not neglect the gift you have, which was given you by prophecy when the council of elders laid their hands on you.

—1 Timothy 4:14

MY FATHER LOST HIS BATTLE WITH CANCER several years ago while I was serving in cross-cultural ministry in Tanzania, East Africa. I was able to travel back to the United States to spend some quality time with him during his final months and later again for his funeral. But I was not in the country when he went to be with his Lord and Savior. I am grateful that my wife-to-be could be with him in my place while he was in his final days of hospice care at home.

I actually met my beautiful wife, a young school teacher, while stateside visiting my father after his cancer diagnosis. We began to be intentional about our relationship before I returned to Tanzania. Though we were not yet formally engaged, our relationship had grown close to a place that my siblings called her to be with my father when it was clear he didn't have much time left.

It was during a moment of clarity after a period of unresponsiveness that my father passed on to her his final message for me. He chose those words well, including the two things every son longs to hear from his father no matter how old he gets. First, that he loved me. Second, that he was proud of the man I'd become.

My father died the very next day. His last words remain very precious to me. As I write them down in this chapter all these years later, I am surprised by the emotional effect they still have on me. We cannot underestimate the power of words. Especially the last words of those we love.

LAST WORDS

The apostle Paul was waiting to be executed by the Roman emperor Nero when he wrote his last words to Timothy. They are very personal and full of encouragement to stay strong in the Lord regardless of the spiritual upheaval and decadence going on all around Timothy. In the pages of 2 Timothy, we can feel Paul's deep concern for his spiritual son, knowing that Timothy will soon be ministering without Paul's fatherly strength and wisdom to guide him. His last words of instruction were as timely for Timothy as they have been for emerging spiritual leaders of every generation.

FAN INTO FLAME THE GIFT OF GOD

Paul doesn't make it too far into this letter before he feels compelled, as fathers often do, to remind his son of the ground they'd already covered (see 1 Timothy 4:14 above). Maybe Timothy didn't quite get it when Paul mentioned it the first time around in his earlier letter. Maybe he had since forgotten. Either way, it was important enough that Paul brings it up again in his subtle command disguised as a reminder: "I remind you to fan into flame the gift of God" (2 Timothy 1:6).

In reading this phrase, two questions will likely arise. First, what is the gift being referenced? Second, how is Timothy supposed to fan this gift into a flame?

41

Let's begin by addressing the first question. Most biblical scholars would agree that "the gift of God" references either a spiritual gift given by God through the Holy Spirit (1 Corinthians 12) or God's giving of the Holy Spirit to believers (Luke 11:13; Acts 2:38-30). While either interpretation is viable, biblical context points to Paul's words referring to a spiritual gift. Specifically, Paul's similar words to Timothy in his prior letter, where it seems clear Paul had already addressed this topic.

> Do not neglect the gift you have, which was given you by prophecy when the council of elders laid their hands on you.
>
> —1 Timothy 4:14

Since the second letter speaks of Timothy's gift coming through Paul's own laying on of hands, it would seem logical that Paul was one of the elders mentioned here in the first letter. If that is the case, then it would seem even more evident that both passages are referring to a specific spiritual gift. From what both letters tell us of Timothy's ministry, his spiritual gift was most likely that of an overseer, what we also term an elder, pastor, or bishop. The great church historian Eusebius (fourth century A.D.), mentions Timothy in this role,[1] and both of Paul's letters to Timothy can easily be read through this lens.

In the next couple chapters, we will be speaking further of spiritual gifts. So it might be profitable to pause now for a closer look at how the Bible defines them. Here is just one listing from the apostle Paul's first letter to the Corinthian church of various gifts of the Spirit.

To each [believer] is given the manifestation of the Spirit for the common good. For to one is given through the Spirit the utterance of wisdom, and to another the utterance of knowledge according to the same Spirit, to another faith by the same Spirit, to another gifts of healing by the one Spirit, to another the working of miracles, to another prophecy, to another the ability to distinguish between spirits, to another various kinds of tongues, to another the interpretation of tongues. All these are empowered by one and the same Spirit, who apportions to each one individually as he wills. (emphasis mine)

—1 Corinthians 12:7-11

If this passage were to be distilled into a one-sentence definition, it might read, "Spiritual gifts refer to a supernatural ability given to a believer by God (Holy Spirit) for the building up of the church body."

RECOGNIZING YOUR GIFT

As I've talked with believers all around the world, several things have become apparent to me. For one, most Christians have a decent understanding of what spiritual gifts are. But even many in ministry don't have a clear idea of their personal spiritual gifts or how they can develop these gifts in service to God and God's church. Many Christians may be using their spiritual gifts without even realizing it. Sadly, many more are not utilizing their gifts at all due to a lack of awareness. Other Christians find themselves frustrated because they are trying to minister outside their giftedness.

There may be a lot of reasons why such is the case. But for the purposes of this book, let's focus on remedying this situation. To help with this, I've included below a simple, hands-on, step-by-step approach for confidently identifying the gift or gifts God has given you to use for his glory.

STEP ONE

In discovering your spiritual gift(s), it is essential to start the process by asking God to give you insight, as the apostle James encouraged anyone lacking understanding to do.

> If any of you lacks wisdom, let him ask God, who gives generously to all without reproach, and it will be given him. But let him ask in faith, with no doubting.
>
> —James 1:5-6a

Ask God to give you the Holy Spirit in abundance so that he is your guide through this journey of discovery. Then believe God will honor this request. After all, the Holy Spirit is the giver of this gift. He wants you to recognize it and use it for his glory and the building up of other believers.

STEP TWO

Study what God's Word has to say about this subject. Some essential passages on spiritual gifts are Romans 12 and 1 Corinthians 12-14. Don't be tempted to run straight to the lists of spiritual gifts these chapters provide. Rather, explore topics that arise within the text:

- Why are we given spiritual gifts?
- Does every believer have a spiritual gift?
- Where do spiritual gifts come from?
- How do I practice my spiritual gift(s) in love?
- Should we seek after some spiritual gifts more than others?

STEP THREE

Once you've studied these topics, it's time to look through the lists of spiritual gifts to see if any of those mentioned connect with who you are or any positive ministry experiences you've had. Keep in mind that these lists don't include all the spiritual gifts that exist, but they are a good place to start.

STEP FOUR

Once you have some idea as to potential spiritual gifts, it would be good to share that list with other Christians in your life to get their insights. Choose believers with a vibrant spiritual walk who also know you well. They will be able to add further clarity and affirmation to your list of potential gifts.

STEP FIVE

After you've received feedback, it's time to consolidate everything you've discovered so far. By this point, at least one or two gifts should have risen to the surface as strong possibilities.

Step Six

Now it's time to "try on" these potential gifts by practicing them and observing carefully where God is most at work as you serve. In the early stages, there is wisdom to finding ministry settings that are low-key and feel safe. As you serve in these areas, you will eventually notice that others are blessed when you practice a certain gift. You may hear statements like, "You should do that again! . . . God really ministered to me through your service! Wow, you are a real natural at that!"

Even if others around you don't give you verbal affirmation, you will probably notice God's blessing on you as you use a particular gift. Such results are good indicators that God is revealing your spiritual gift to you.

Once we have clearly identified the gifts God has given us, we can begin to grow confidently in them through purposeful development and use. In the following chapters, we will see that these gifts come with an obligation to do just that. They weren't given to us by the Holy Spirit to be put on a shelf and admired but to be used for the "common good" of our faith communities (1 Corinthians 12:7). As believers discover and own their gifts in this way, Christ's universal Church will see a dramatic increase in the Holy Spirit's grace and power.

Reflect and Apply

What new insights or affirmations have you received in regard to your spiritual giftedness?

CHAPTER FIVE

REMEMBERING TO KEEP GOD'S GIFTS ABLAZE

Therefore, I remind you to **keep ablaze the gift of God** *that is in you through the laying on of my hands. (emphasis mine)*

—*2 Timothy 1:6 (HSCB)*

WITH A BETTER UNDERSTANDING OF WHAT spiritual gifts are, we will now address the second question. How exactly do we fan our gift into a flame? Or as the Holman Christian Standard Bible (HCSB) translates this phrase (see above), how do we *keep our gift ablaze*?

This is an important question because spiritual gifts, like fires, will grow cold if we don't maintain them properly. It's one thing to start a fire. It's another thing altogether to keep a healthy fire ablaze. This takes intentionality and focus as anyone who has ever sat around a campfire can testify. Even before a fire is lit, enough wood must be gathered to last the evening. This wood must be dry, cut to the proper sizes, and stacked an appropriate distance from the fire, close enough to be within reach but not so close as to catch on fire prematurely.

Once everything is prepared and the fire lit, then comes the work of tending the fire. This may seem straightforward, but it's easy to get so caught up talking with friends and family that we forget to stir the embers and add more wood until the fire is almost dead. When we're distracted, even by good things, it's easy to let fires grow cold. This is why Paul reminded Timothy in his first letter:

> Do not neglect the gift you have, which was given you by prophecy when the council of elders laid their hands on you.
>
> —1 Timothy 4:14

FORGETTING TO USE OUR SPIRITUAL GIFTS IS NEGLIGENCE

The first way to keep a spiritual gift ablaze is to not get so busy with other "pressing matters" we forget to practice it. While we may know this, it doesn't always translate into us living this truth. Even those who know their spiritual gifts and have an understanding of their responsibility to use them can find themselves not engaging as they should in their gifts because they are saying yes to too many other things. Life and ministry both hold so many demands. The constant temptation is to feel we have to do it all.

In reality, there can often be a sinful element to this where we actually enjoy being a "one man" or "one woman" show. Whether it's a need to be in control or feel needed, we take on responsibilities to which we have no business saying yes. As our responsibilities increase, so does our busyness. What this really comes down to is learning to be content with the boundaries God has chosen for us, as King David expressed beautifully in one of his psalms.

> The Lord is my chosen portion and my cup; you hold my lot. The lines have fallen for me in pleasant places; indeed, I have a beautiful inheritance.
>
> —Psalm 16:5-6

The problem is when we don't see God's boundary lines as the protective gifts they are but as restrictions that hold us back. Our attention is divided among way too many things. Maybe we've bought into the lie that to be relevant in this modern age, or even just to survive in it, we have to live and minister at a frantic pace.

In reality, we decide every day to say yes to some activities. Every time we do that, we are by default saying no to everything else. Regardless of what we believe our priorities to be, how we spend our time, money, and emotions indicates what we value most. Everything else, the things we value less, get what is left over.

Applying this to our spiritual gifts, it doesn't matter how important we say stewarding our spiritual gifts is to us. If we are neglecting to use those gifts, they really aren't a priority, plain and simple. Once we own this truth, we can take an honest look at our lives and prayerfully consider what we should be saying no to so that we can say yes to stewarding well the gifts that God has given us.

FEARING TO USE OUR SPIRITUAL GIFTS IS NEGLIGENCE

Fear is another reason we often find ourselves neglecting the fires of our spiritual gifts. This was the very reason Timothy was holding back from fully engaging in his gift of overseer. As part of his ministry, he was responsible to instruct and even correct the older men and women of his church. In his first letter to Timothy, we see that Paul needed to implore Timothy to fulfill his responsibilities even if that meant correcting an elder of the church.

> As for [elders] who persist in sin, rebuke them in the presence of all, so that the rest may stand in fear. In the presence of God and of Christ Jesus and of the elect angels I charge you to keep these rules without prejudging, doing nothing from partiality.
>
> —1 Timothy 5:20-21

Paul was very clear here that Timothy must fulfill even the uncomfortable responsibilities that came with his spiritual gift. But earlier in the same passage, Paul also coaches Timothy on how to handle this delicate situation.

> **Do not rebuke an older man but encourage him as you would a father**, younger men as brothers, **older women as mothers**, younger women as sisters, in all purity. (emphasis mine)
>
> —1 Timothy 5:1

Some Bible versions translate this passage as "do not harshly rebuke" because the Greek word here for rebuke conveys the image of punching someone verbally. In other words, when Timothy approached older Christians of his community with church discipline issues, whether men or women, he was not to be combative or overly harsh with his words. This is something many of us are prone to do when we try to overcompensate for our own fears and insecurities.

It's easy to look down on Timothy for being timid as he practiced his spiritual gift. But I for one have often held back from doing what needs to be done out of fear of the response I might receive. At one point while a missionary in Tanzania, I was given a leadership position over a number of missionary team leaders serving all over the African continent. These leaders came from different regions of the world, but what they all had in common was a love for God and a desire to see unreached people groups know him. This often required ministering in very rugged conditions among people groups historically resistant to the gospel.

It takes a special person to lead a multi-national team in these kinds of situations. By special, I mean that they were usually a blend of godliness, stubbornness, and toughness. I've always respected people like this—from afar! Up close, they can be hard to lead. I'll admit I was often intimidated and just a little tempted to leave well enough alone. Especially with those who'd been serving God on the African continent longer than I'd been alive. It was easy for me to push off hard conversations to another day.

But God impressed on me that for the sake of these leaders, the teams they oversaw, and the lost people to whom they ministered, I had to step up if the way they were leading was either unwise or in direct opposition to scriptural leadership principles. Healthy confrontation even for the good of others doesn't come naturally to me. But I am purposefully growing in this area because I know being a good leader means putting other people's growth above my own desire to be liked and respected.

This is the same conviction we need to have in using our spiritual gifts. We don't practice them because it's comfortable. We practice them because this brings glory to God and it is how we build up our fellow believers.

REFLECT AND APPLY

Do you find that you are not using your spiritual gift due to negligence or fear? What do you need to do to more fully engage in your gift(s)?

CHAPTER SIX
PRACTICING YOUR GIFTS WITH PURPOSE

For this reason I remind you to fan into flame the gift of God, which is in you through the laying on of my hands.

—2 Timothy 1:6

Practice these things; immerse yourself in them, so that all may see your progress.

—1 Timothy 4:15

AN OCCASIONAL LOG THROWN ON A FIRE may keep it going. But it does little towards growing a healthy flame. It is important to identify and use our spiritual gifts. But we can't be content to stop there. To continue progressing in the gift entrusted to us, we need to look at the same three elements Paul gives Timothy in the above verse (1 Timothy 4:15).

- Practice these things.
- Immerse yourself in them.
- So that all may see your progress.

The gifts we receive from the Holy Spirit are not something we earn but something we steward. Developing any resource we've been given to its fullest potential takes a lot of effort and intentionality. The renowned South African Christian pastor, teacher, and author Andrew Murray expressed it like this in his title *The Ministry of Intercessory Prayer.*

> Unless we are willing to pay the price, to sacrifice time and attention for seemingly legitimate or necessary tasks for the sake of the spiritual gifts, we need not look for much power from above in our work.

With Murray's words in mind, let's take a look at the three elements Paul gives Timothy in the above verse and three **progress principles** for practicing our gifts that we can extract from his words, each essential for purposefully developing our spiritual gifts so we can use them with power.

PROGRESS PRINCIPLE #1: PRACTICING WITH PRAYER PRODUCES LASTING FRUIT

Being a good steward of your gift means doing your part to ensure it is producing eternal fruit. The most important thing you can do in this regard is to practice your gift with prayer. Bathing your gift in prayer allows the Holy Spirit's power to be in you as you practice it. This in turn guards you from using your gift in your own strength, which will not produce lasting fruit. The apostle Paul warns us that any work done in our own strength will not survive the day of God's judgment.

> For no one can lay a foundation other than that which is laid, which is Jesus Christ. Now if anyone builds on the foundation with gold, silver, precious stones, wood, hay, straw—each one's work will become manifest, for the Day will disclose it, because it will be revealed by fire, and the fire will test what sort of work each one has done. If the work that anyone has built on the foundation [of Christ] survives, he will receive a reward. If anyone's work is burned up, he will suffer loss, though he himself will be saved, but only as through fire.
>
> —1 Corinthians 3:11-15

If we want to produce works built on Christ that don't burn up like "wood, hay, and stubble," it is imperative we use our gift under the Holy Spirit's authority. He is the one who has given us our gift. He is the one who will guide and empower us as we use it. We will be further addressing the Holy Spirit's indwelling and power in a later chapter.

PROGRESS PRINCIPLE #2: GODLY GUIDANCE PRODUCES GROWTH AND GRACE

Another vital progress principle is to practice your spiritual gift under the instruction of a mature sister or brother in the Lord who has the same gift but has developed it further. This could be through any combination of ministry partnerships, mentorships, workshops, podcasts, or books. We live in a blessed age when a plethora of learning resources are readily available just a click or two away. It would be poor stewardship not to capitalize on modern technology and glean from the expertise of others.

But nothing replaces life-on-life mentorship to encourage deep spiritual growth alongside gift development. This could range from something as simple as volunteering in a church or local outreach ministry under more experienced volunteers to a formal ministry apprenticeship to joining a ministry full-time under oversight of appointed team or staff leadership. Later in his second letter to Timothy, Paul charges Timothy in how to use his gift of overseer.

> Preach the word; be ready in season and out of season: reprove, rebuke, and exhort, with complete patience and teaching.
>
> —2 Timothy 4:2

Notice that most of Paul's charge deals with tasks that fall under Timothy's spiritual gift as an overseer. But Paul ends his instruction by challenging Timothy to use his gift with "complete patience." Patience is one of the fruits of the Spirit.

> But the fruit of the Spirit is love, joy, peace, **patience**, kindness, goodness, faithfulness, gentleness, self-control. (emphasis mine)
>
> —Galatians 5:22-23a

As Paul mentored Timothy, he both modeled in person and encouraged by letter the importance of using the gifts of the Spirit in conjunction with the fruits of the Spirit. This is the beauty of developing our gifts under the tutelage of mature believers. As we serve under them, we not only grow in our gifts but we also grow in grace.

PROGRESS PRINCIPLE #3: BLESSING OTHERS BRINGS GOD'S BLESSINGS

The last progress principle is a simple but profound one. The more you bless others with your spiritual gift, the more God will bless your spiritual gift. This is the way it works with all resources in God's kingdom. The more we use them for God's glory and the edification of others, the more the Father heaps them on us. Jesus said as much in his Sermon on the Mount discourse.

> Give and it will be given to you. Good measure, pressed down, shaken together, running over, will be put into your lap. For with the measure you use, it will be measured back to you.
>
> —Luke 6:38

This verse really captures the abundant way God promises to bless us as we bless others. But the imagery of using a measure, pressing down, shaking together, etc., is not as common today. So maybe this promise doesn't impact you as profoundly as it would have Jesus's original listeners. For a fuller picture of what Jesus was saying in this verse, let's go to the Old Testament book of Ruth. This very short historical account of just four chapters is an unlikely love story between an older, highly-respected Jewish man and a younger Moabite woman, widow of a Jewish man, whose eventual marriage would end up producing the family line of King David and ultimately Jesus.

At one point in the story, the older Jewish man, Boaz, wants to send the young Moabite woman, Ruth, off with a gift.

> And he said, "Bring the garment you are wearing and hold it out." So she [Ruth] held it, and he measured out six measures of barley and put it on her.
>
> —Ruth 3:15

In this scene, Boaz was doing exactly what Jesus described in his promise of blessing. Boaz was measuring out grain into the "lap" of Ruth's garment, which would have been a loose gown tied around her waist by a sash. Think of a pioneer-age woman or even early twentieth-century farmwife gathering eggs by depositing them in the gathered-up front of her skirt or apron. In customary Middle Eastern hospitality, Boaz would have made a show of his affections by pouring as much grain as he could into his measuring cups, then adding even more on top until her garment overflowed. This is the abundant way God blesses when we use our resources like spiritual gifts to bless others.

WHEN OTHERS SEE YOUR PROGRESS

Notice the last of the three elements Paul mentioned above to Timothy: "So that all may see your progress" (1 Timothy 4:15). As you immerse yourself in your spiritual gift and practice it with purpose, others will indeed see your progress. This is a blessed position to be in, but it is also a very precarious one. The temptation can be to see our spiritual gift as a way to bring attention to ourselves. If this happens, then we've completely lost focus on the purpose for which God has given us our gifts. This is an easy trap to fall into because we are all prone to pride. This is why Paul warned Timothy against appointing church overseers/elders who were new converts.

> He [church leaders] must not be a recent convert, or he may become puffed up with conceit and fall into the condemnation of the devil.
>
> —1 Timothy 3:6

New Christians rarely have the spiritual maturity to resist the prideful temptations that come with leadership and fruitful ministries. Sadly, this applies to many older Christians as well. Paul tells us in this warning that when we give into pride, we fall under the condemnation of the devil, who was the first to look at the gifts God gave him and fall into this sin.

The word Paul uses for "puffed up" in this verse has its roots in the Greek word *typotheis*, used to describe a cloud of smoke rising from a smoldering fire. This is the kind of smoke we give off when our Holy Spirit fires start to smolder due to pride. This "puffed up" smoke often draws a lot of flattering attention, which only increases our pride issues because everyone, including ourselves, thinks a lot of smoke means a big, healthy fire. In reality, all that smothering smoke billowing around us is evidence that our fire is choking and dying out.

Fires that are just getting started and those that are dying out often look a lot alike. It takes a discerning eye to know the difference. But one thing you can know without being a fire expert is that hotly burning, efficient fires usually put out very little smoke for others to notice. If we are using our gifts for God's glory, neither should we.

REFLECT AND APPLY

As you progress in your spiritual gifts, what can you implement now to help you safeguard against the desire to seek a crown instead of God's glory?

CHAPTER SEVEN
PAYING CLOSE ATTENTION TO YOUR LIFE

For this reason I remind you to fan into flame the gift of God, which is in you through the laying on of my hands.

—*2 Timothy 1:6*

Pay close attention to your life and your teaching; persevere in these things, for by doing this you will save both yourself and your hearers.

—*1 Timothy 4:16*

IT'S EASY TO THINK THAT BECAUSE GOD HAS BLESSED our gift in the past, then this equates to a strong spiritual life in the present. This is a fatal error that can be brought on by pride. But it can also happen when we forget Paul's warning in his first letter to Timothy to "pay close attention to your life" (see 1 Timothy 4:16 above).

This verse is a challenge to stay vigilant in our walk with God even as we minister with our spiritual gifts. There have been too many prominent men and women of God whose private lives fell apart even while their spiritual gifts were still shining bright. They mistook shine for substance and in the process neglected the source of their gift. Jesus addressed this problem using the analogy of a grapevine.

> I am the vine; you are the branches. Whoever abides in me and I in him,
> he it is that bears much fruit, for apart from me you can do nothing. If
> anyone does not abide in me, he is thrown away like a branch and withers;
> and the branches are gathered, thrown into the fire, and burned.
>
> —John 15:5-6

In this analogy, Jesus identified himself as the vine and his followers as the branches. Only inasmuch as we remain connected to him will we bear spiritual fruit. If we aren't connected, we will simply dry up and wither away, good for nothing but kindling to be tossed in the fire and burned. Of course, a grape branch separated from the vine doesn't wilt away instantaneously to a twig after being cut. Likewise, we usually don't notice we are spiritually withered up until we are cut off and it's too late.

Regardless of how spiritually healthy a person appears to be, the reality is that they will produce fruit in direct correlation to how connected they are with Christ. The deeper our connection to Christ, the more ablaze our lives will be for him and the more his Spirit will produce everlasting fruit through us as we use our spiritual gifts. Nineteenth-century American clergyman and Christian author E.M. Bounds noted in his work *Power through Prayer.* "To be little with God is to be little for God." We could say the opposite of this is true as well: "To be much with God is to be much for God."

So how exactly do we pay attention to our lives? Paul tells us in the second half of his warning to Timothy.

Pay close attention to your life and your teaching; **persevere in these things, for by doing this you will save both yourself and your hearers.** (emphasis mine)

—1 Timothy 4:16, HCSB

It is important to understand that Paul is not suggesting here that Timothy will earn salvation for himself and his congregants as he uses his spiritual gift. Paul is reminding Timothy that his ability to live for God and the ability of his congregation depends on keeping his own fire ablaze even if those around him are sliding into heresy and moral decay. Paul knows that Timothy as a spiritual leader is responsible to keep ablaze the fire of his spiritual community.

In ancient cultures, fire was highly valued, not only for its practical uses but also for its symbolism and spiritual significance. We now live in a world where many of our fireplaces come with electronic igniters. If we are roughing it, we may have to use a butane lighter or even an old-fashioned match. All of these are relatively new inventions on the human scene. Fire used to be something hard-to-come-by while vital for maintaining a healthy existence.

Because of this, many ancient cultures, tribes, and villages would have a fire that was always kept burning. The person who tended this fire was responsible for keeping it alive along with performing any rituals that went with their unique role. One such ancient culture was the First Nation Peoples of North America, who lived on that continent's great plains and plateaus.

These semi-nomadic people groups would travel on a yearly migration path, following their primary food source, the ever-roaming bison. While this nomadic lifestyle provided almost all of their needs, it did have some drawbacks. One was the difficult task of getting fires going every time they set up a new camp. This process was so intensive and technical, they even created the following legend about it.

One day, Coyote, always the trickster in the animal kingdom, got up the nerve to steal fire from three witches. As the witches gave chase, Coyote passed the fire to another forest animal, who in turn passed it on to another. In this way, the fire passed from animal to animal until it finally ended up in the possession of an old frog, who got cornered by the witches. In desperation, the frog spit the fire into a tree stump, which hid the fire by swallowing it. Because of this, according to the legend, you can get fire from a tree if you know how to properly ask for it.[1]

Of course, this legend can be connected back historically to indigenous peoples cleverly harvesting burning wood from a forest fire or other wildfires. But instead of every lodge "asking the tree for fire" when they got to a new camp, i.e., having to start a fire laboriously from scratch, these First Nation tribal groups appointed a fire keeper to keep an "eternal flame" for each community. This person was responsible to carry the coals of the "eternal flame" from camp to camp in a special horn or bundle of sage bark.[2] When everyone reached their new camp, the fire keeper would bring this flame back to life. Then each family could light their own fire from this central fire.

In many ways, the "eternal flame" was the fire keeper's personal fire since he was the one who carried it and kept it going. At the same time, he knew he was keeping this fire for something beyond himself. He was keeping it for the good of the entire community, who knew with certainty there would always be at least one place they could go to get live embers. For a fire keeper to let his fire go out could mean plunging the entire community into cold and darkness. When he faithfully kept his personal fire going, this ensured warmth and light for every lodge.

In this indigenous culture, only one person in each wandering tribal group was responsible to keep the eternal flame going. As Christ's people, we are all called on to keep our faith, spiritual gifts, and ministry burning in our lives. This is a call for every believer, but it is especially true for those God has put into spiritual leadership positions.

Without a doubt, it is essential for spiritual leaders to keep their personal flames burning for the benefit of their own spiritual health and ministries. But Paul also makes clear to Timothy that good leaders need to understand that their lives and ministries aren't only about them. Perhaps even more important should be the weight of knowing that their communities, whose own flames are constantly being threatened, are depending on their spiritual leaders to keep their "eternal fire" ablaze so that spiritual cold and darkness does not descend on them.

REFLECT AND APPLY

As Paul encouraged Timothy to pay close attention to his spiritual life, we too need to keep our personal flames ablaze. Reflect on the health of your eternal flame. What do you need to do in order to stoke the fire so that it continues to burn bright?

Chapter Eight
Paying Close Attention to Your Gifts

Practice these things; be committed to them, so that your progress may be evident to all. Pay close attention to your life and your teaching; persevere in these things, for by doing this you will save both yourself and your hearers.

—*1 Timothy 4:16 (HCSB)*

O Timothy, guard the deposit entrusted to you. Avoid the irreverent babble and contradictions of what is falsely called "knowledge" for by professing it some have swerved from the faith.

—*1 Timothy 6:20-21*

IN 1 TIMOTHY 4:16, WE'VE SEEN THAT PAUL not only challenges Timothy to pay close attention to his life but also encourages him to stay focused on his teaching. False teachers in and around Ephesus were peddling a gospel that, on the surface at least, appeared more attractive than the true gospel message Timothy was teaching. These false teachers claimed additional divine knowledge that gave them license to live out "their own passions" (2 Timothy 4:3). Because of their superior communication skills and the authority they projected, such teachers had been leading many people astray within the early church. In defending his ministry to the church in Corinth, the apostle Paul sarcastically termed some of these false teachers "super-apostles."

> For if someone comes and proclaims another Jesus than the one we proclaimed, or . . . a different gospel from the one you accepted, you put up with it readily enough. Indeed, I consider that I am not in the least inferior to these **super-apostles**. Even if I am unskilled in speaking, I am not so in knowledge. (emphasis mine)
>
> —2 Corinthians 11:4-6a

If such a well-respected early church leader as the apostle Paul could have his ministry brought into question by the Corinthian church because of errant teachers, it is certainly likely that Timothy's ministry in Ephesus was also under pressure. Paul urges Timothy to avoid such "irreverent babble," contradictions, and supposed special knowledge but instead to remain focused on the spiritual gift of ministry the Holy Spirit had deposited within him (see 1 Timothy 6:20-21 above). If Timothy allowed himself to get distracted by these "successful" people or cave in to the pressures they put on him, he'd be doing his church a major disservice, wandering away from the true gospel and leading them astray in the process.

Similarly as we practice our gifts in ministry, we shouldn't be tempted to mimic or give homage to other "successful ministers" who peddle anything less than the gospel of Christ. This will not bode well for us or those we serve. Which raises another important point regarding spiritual gifts we might prefer to ignore but nevertheless need to consider since this issue is taught clearly in Scripture. The plain truth is that God blesses some people with greater portions of gifts than others.

> But grace was given to each one of us according to the measure of Christ's gift.
>
> —Ephesians 4:7

> Having gifts that differ according to the grace given to us, let us use them.
>
> —Romans 12:6

This truth is portrayed clearly in one of numerous parables Jesus used to teach his disciples. Found in Matthew 25, the Parable of the Talents unpacks kingdom stewardship principles through the symbolic story of a wealthy master going on a journey and leaving the care of his home to his employees.

> For it will be like a man going on a journey, who called his servants and entrusted to them his property. To one he gave five talents, to another two, to another one, to each according to his ability. Then he went away. He who had received the five talents went at once and traded with them, and he made five talents more. So also he who had the two talents made two talents more.
>
> —Matthew 25:14-17

In this story, the wealthy traveler symbolizes Jesus. The servants he leaves in charge during his absence symbolize his disciples. It is important to note that "talent" in this passage doesn't refer to natural abilities but the largest unit of money in this time period, equivalent to six thousand denarii. One denarius (singular form) in turn represented a day's wages for a hired laborer. In other words, this master was entrusting huge sums of money to these servants, not to just go out and spend but to invest on their master's behalf.

If you read the rest of the parable, you will discover that the two servants who'd doubled their master's money (symbolizing physical/spiritual resources) were termed "good and faithful" and rewarded greatly. The third servant was so afraid he might lose his investment that he just hid his single talent, ultimately incurring his master's displeasure and loss of reward. This parable contains many stewardship principles, but I want to focus only on the statement that "to one he gave five talents, to another two, to another one, **to each according to his ability**" (v. 15).

We are typically taught from childhood that every human being is "created equal," so that last phrase may bother us. But real life also teaches us quickly that not all of us are equally gifted with the same abilities or to the same degree. I might wish to be an NBA basketball player, but God didn't give me the same height or coordination as Michael Jordan. As our creator and the giver of all good gifts, it is God's prerogative to distribute both natural abilities and spiritual gifts as he sees fit.

This was a hard truth for me to accept. But once I came to grips with it, I was able to experience a freedom that allowed me to use my own specific God-bestowed gifts in a one-of-a-kind way that no one but me could. Let me share how I learned that lesson in hopes that you won't have to learn it the hard way as I did.

In my early twenties, I went on my first long-term mission assignment abroad. New to all things missions, I joined a team of other new missionaries-in-training. Since I was single, I was assigned to share a house with another single male teammate from my home country. This young man seemed to excel effortlessly at everything. He was an incredibly gifted language learner, very personable, an engaging teacher, and had musical talents as well.

Meanwhile, I struggled to learn a new language, adapt to a new culture, and navigate a new life. Up to this point in my life, I'd been used to success. Not because I was particularly bright or talented. In fact, one could make a case for the opposite. Still, I'd found a lot of success by simply being very driven at anything to which I put my mind.

But in that particular cross-cultural ministry setting, I just couldn't seem to thrive no matter how hard I tried. In many areas, I was barely surviving. It was a perfect storm for me to become distracted and bitter, which is exactly what I did. I spent more time obsessing about all the things this missions "superstar" could do than just faithfully doing whatever God placed in front of me each day.

At some point well into my experience, God used John 21 to convict me about my sinful obsession. In this passage, the resurrected Jesus is on a post-breakfast walk with his disciples by the Sea of Galilee. During their stroll, Jesus purposefully broke away from the group to have a much-needed talk with Peter. Jesus knew that Peter needed some forgiveness and closure for denying him three times while being questioned by the high priest (Matthew 26; John 18). So he asked Peter to declare his love for Jesus—one time for each denial.

Having put this hard but necessary conversation behind them, Jesus then told Peter he'd get another opportunity to relive that infamous moment and prove his love for him by the manner of his death. Jesus then added two life-changing words: "Follow me" (v. 19).

Where was Jesus asking Peter to follow him? Ultimately, to Peter's death on a Roman cross, the very agonizing fate that had struck so much fear into his heart on the day he'd chosen to deny his friend and Savior rather than risk such a death. When Peter heard this prophecy of how he would die, he immediately turned around and looked at his co-disciple and friend John, who was following close behind.

"Lord, what about this man?" he asked.

Jesus replied (my paraphrase): "What I do with John is between John and me, and that is none of your business. Your business is to follow me!"

This story cut me to the core. It was the hard but loving message from God I desperately needed to hear. What God was doing in and through my teammate's gifts and ministry was between the two of them, and it was none of my business. My business was to follow Jesus in the unique way he was asking me alone to do. This freed me from the unrealistic expectations I'd put on myself to be something I wasn't and allowed me to get on with serving God the way he'd created me to do. It also allowed me to enjoy a real friendship with this teammate.

When we compare our gifts to others, one of two things happen. If we are the less gifted person, we get super discouraged and self-focused. If we have the greater portion of giftedness, we become super prideful and self-focused. Either way, we lose and Satan wins because we are full of self and distracted. What has started as an unhealthy distraction towards others has now become a prideful obsession with self.

If you focus on the fact that others out there will inevitably have greater portions of various gifts than you, it will destroy your ministry. Instead, you must rejoice because God has not only created you uniquely but also has good works that you alone were designed to carry out.

For we are his workmanship, created in Christ Jesus for good works, which God prepared beforehand, that we should walk in them.

—Ephesians 2:10

As Paul reminded Timothy, when you practice your God-bestowed gifts and are committed fully to using them for God's kingdom, your progress will become evident to others (1 Timothy 4:15). Like the faithful servants in the Parable of the Talents, you will find that God himself will increase the portion and influence of those gifts. This is the process God uses to keep your life and spiritual gifts ablaze for his glory.

REFLECT AND APPLY

As you use your gifts, are you comparing yourself to anyone else? If so, how is this holding you back from doing the works God created specifically for you?

GOING DEEPER

SUGGESTED ACTIVITIES

1. Rearrange your schedule by saying no to things that do not further your spiritual gifts, which will free up time to say yes to opportunities that allow you to use and develop your gifts.

2. Find a mature believer with your spiritual gift(s) from whom you can learn.

3. Find someone in whom you see evidence of your own spiritual gift(s) who you in turn can encourage and bring alongside to learn from you.

4. Read John 21, then go on a walk with Jesus while meditating on what it means for you personally to obey Jesus's command: "Follow me."

SUGGESTED READING:

Understanding Spiritual Gifts: A Comprehensive Guide by Sam Storms

Section Three:
Gifts from Our Father

O my Father! There is nothing I desire so much as to be filled with the Holy Spirit. The blessings He brings are so unspeakable. They are just what I need. He fills the heart with Your love and with Yourself. I long for this! He breathes the mind and life of Christ into me, so that I can live as He did, in and for the Father's love. I long for this! He supplies power from heaven for all my walk and work. I long for this! O Father! Please give me the fullness of Your Spirit today. Father! I base this request on the words of my Lord: "How much more will He give the Holy Spirit." I believe that You hear my prayer, and that I receive now just what I am asking for. Father! I claim and I take it! The fullness of Your Spirit is mine. I receive this gift today as a faith gift. In faith, I believe the Father works everything He has promised through the Spirit. The Father delights in breathing His Spirit into His waiting child as he fellowships with Him. Amen.

—Pastor Andrew Murray
South African clergyman, nineteenth century

CHAPTER NINE
GOD HAS NOT GIVEN US A SPIRIT OF COWARDLINESS

For God gave us a spirit not of fear but of power and love and self-control.

—*2 Timothy 1:7*

ONE OF THE FIRST NEGATIVE EMOTIONS documented in human history was unhealthy fear. The very first documented emotion was shame. But even shame is really a derivative of fear. For what is shame but being afraid that people will see us as we truly are and that we will fall short of their expectations? The catalyst for these first two negative emotions was humanity's first sin.

> So when the woman saw that the tree was good for food, and that it was a delight to the eyes, and that the tree was to be desired to make one wise, she took of its fruit and ate, and she also gave some to her husband who was with her, and he ate. Then the eyes of both were opened, and they knew that they were naked. And they sewed fig leaves together and made themselves loincloths. And they heard the sound of the Lord God walking in the garden in the cool of the day, and the man and his wife hid themselves from the presence of the Lord God among the trees of the garden. But the Lord God called to the man and said to him, "Where are you?" And he said, "I heard the sound of you in the garden, and **I was afraid, because I was naked**, and I hid myself." (emphasis added)
>
> —Genesis 3:6-10

The context of this story is the creation of the first man and woman, Adam and Eve. God placed them in the garden of Eden and gave them total freedom to eat whatever they wanted except for the fruit of "the tree of the knowledge of good and evil" (Genesis 2:16). The consequence of eating from this tree would be death. Adam and Eve ended up doing the one thing God told them not to do, placing them and the world they were tasked to care for under the curse of sin and death (Romans 5:12).

Notice that their instinctive reactions in this newly chosen life of death come from a place of shame and fear. First, Adam and Eve realized they were naked, so they made loin cloths to hide their shame from each other. Then they hid behind trees in fear of God. Ever since that moment, humanity has been hiding from God, from others, and from themselves.

As a physical descendant of our first parents, Timothy would have inherited their curse of sin and death just as we all do. Each of us struggles with sin and fear in this life. Some of Paul's instructions to Timothy in both letters would seem to indicate that Timothy's own fears may have manifested when trying to confront well-established and older church leadership who were promoting a false gospel. We've already examined Paul's directive to avoid contentious babble and false knowledge (1 Timothy 6:20-21). Paul reinforces this when he tells Timothy why he is leaving him in leadership at this particular church.

> Remain at Ephesus so that you may charge certain persons not to teach any different doctrine, nor to devote themselves to myths and endless genealogies, which promote speculations rather than the stewardship from God that is by faith.
>
> —1 Timothy 1:3b-4

In the same letter, Paul encourages Timothy to "let no one despise you for your youth, but set the believers an example" (1 Timothy 4: 12). We examined earlier how Paul goes on to instruct Timothy that in confronting older church members, he should approach them with respect as he would a father or mother (1 Timothy 5:1).

Timothy may not have been chronologically equal to these problematic church leaders, but Paul knew he was more mature spiritually. As such, Timothy needed to step up and lead them by preaching God's Word and living it out in front of them. Still, it would be natural for Timothy to hold back out of fear of inevitable confrontation from this older but errant generation. This is why Paul reminded Timothy that God didn't give us a "spirit of fear" (2 Timothy 1:7). Under sin's curse, it would be natural to feel fear in this situation, but such fear was not from God. Timothy needed to put his fears aside so he could do what Paul and God were asking him to do.

It should be noted that Paul, who was telling Timothy not to fear, was far from a stranger to fear himself. In the book of Acts, we see a pattern to Paul's ministry. As he traveled to new places, he used whatever situation was available to preach the gospel. In consequence of his Holy Spirit-filled ministry, many people turned to Christ. This typically led to a major fallout with local religious and political leaders, followed by serious persecution.

When Paul first preached to the Corinthians, the local synagogue leader Crispus along with many others believed in Christ (Acts 18). As in other cities, the religious leaders "opposed and reviled him" (v. 6). After prior experiences, Paul was probably bracing himself for the usual fallout of stoning, beatings, and imprisonment. He may even have been planning to move on to another city. It was at this point that God came to Paul in a vision, telling him:

> Don't be afraid, but go on speaking and do not be silent, for I am with you, and no one will attack you to harm you.
>
> —Acts 18:9-10a

Paul listened to God and stayed on in Corinth for another eighteen months, teaching and encouraging the new believers. We see in these various Scripture passages that Paul and Timothy both experienced the emotion of fear but in two very unique ways. In the English translation, the word *fear* is used in both Acts 18:9-10 and 2 Timothy 1:7. But in the original Greek, these are two different words that give a clearer picture of what kind of fears Paul and Timothy were experiencing.

When God tells Paul, "Don't be afraid," the Greek word used is *phobou,* referring to a general fear, the word from which we get our English word *phobia.* But when Paul tells Timothy that God hasn't given us a spirit of fear, the Greek word used is *deilias,* which refers to a cowardly fear. This is the fear seen when a soldier drops his shield and weapons to run from the battlefield. It is a paralyzing fear that robs us of courage and holds us back from doing what needs to be done. As believers, it's what keeps us from stepping out in obedience to Christ.

Nelson Mandela, South Africa's political-prisoner-turned-president, learned that true courage comes as we learn to push through this debilitating fear so common to us all. He once stated:

I learned that courage was not the absence of fear but the triumph over it. The brave man is not he who does not feel afraid but he who conquers that fear.

—Nelson Mandela

Healthy fear is not a bad thing. In fact, it's a gift from God that helps keep us from danger and death. As I write this chapter, I am living in a large city in the Middle East. Because I don't have a car, I often have to walk places that involve crossing major boulevards with up to four or five lanes of traffic whizzing by in both directions. I've noticed an interesting phenomenon that happens as people cross these busy avenues. Pedestrians will actually walk straight out across the path of oncoming cars, which make no effort to stop for them.

If everything works out right, the pedestrians will have timed this to find themselves beyond each lane of cars as it flows past. This works beautifully millions of times every day. But when it doesn't, it ends very badly for both the pedestrians and vehicles involved. Since I've seen the aftermath of a miscalculation, I feel a tinge of fear in my chest every time I step out into the rushing traffic.

This is a healthy form of fear. It's what keeps me alert and focused so that I can make it to the other side of the street in one piece. This kind of fear is a warning signal from God, and there is nothing cowardly about it. The only problem would be if I let it keep me from ever crossing the street or if it led me to freeze up in fear halfway across.

Recognizing the difference between normal healthy fear and the kind that holds us back from fully serving God is very important. In 2 Timothy

1:7, Paul isn't telling his young disciple that we should never feel fear but that we shouldn't allow a spirit of cowardliness into our lives. Why? Because if we are believers, then God has given us another very different Spirit as we will see in the next chapter.

REFLECT AND APPLY

What do you think about the concept of healthy and unhealthy fear? How have you seen fear impact your life in both positive and negative ways?

Chapter Ten

God Has Given Us a Spirit of Power

For God gave us a spirit not of fear but of power . . .

—2 Timothy 1:7

By the Holy Spirit who dwells within us, guard the good deposit entrusted to you.

—2 Timothy 1:14

WHAT IS THE "GOOD DEPOSIT" PAUL TELLS TIMOTHY to guard in the above verse? We've already seen that it is the spiritual gift of ministry given to Timothy by the Holy Spirit when Paul and other elders laid hands on him (1 Timothy 4:14; 2 Timothy 1:6). Paul instructs Timothy to guard this deposit by means of the Holy Spirit who dwells within him. Why then did Paul need to remind Timothy not to have a spirit of fear but a spirit of power, i.e., the Holy Spirit?

Because **having** the Holy Spirit didn't mean that Timothy was **full** of the Holy Spirit. When we are full of the Holy Spirit, God transforms us from weak, cowardly people into powerful, courageous men and women of God. Paul was reminding Timothy that you can't be full of fear and full of the Holy Spirit at the same time. The presence of one always means the absence of the other.

FROM COWARD TO COURAGEOUS

The apostle Peter is a great example of the transformation from coward to courageous that happens as the Holy Spirit fills our lives. We see Peter's cowardly nature surface when he denies Christ three times (Matthew 26:57-75). Matthew's account describes how Peter followed at a distance when Jesus was taken to the high priest's palace. What stood out to me in this account was that Peter's first denial wasn't addressed to a temple guard or the high priest but to a servant girl who had made the simple observation, "You also were with Jesus the Galilean" (v. 69). This brief interaction causes

Peter to be seized with fear and deny his Lord and Savior. This is an example of cowardly fear.

Just a few months after Christ's death, resurrection, and ascension to heaven, both Peter and the apostle John were arrested and brought before the religious rulers and high priest, partly because of a miraculous healing they'd performed but mainly because of their preaching about Jesus. This situation would have been far more intimidating than Peter's encounter with the servant girl. The very powerful people responsible for putting Jesus to death were now demanding, "By what power or in what name have you done this?" (Acts 4:7). As Peter takes a breath to speak, one might wonder if he is planning to once again deny his Savior. Let's read how he responds.

> Then Peter was filled with the Holy Spirit and said to them, "Rulers of the people and elders. If we are being examined today about a good deed done to a disabled man by what means he was healed let it be known to all of you and to all the people of Israel, that by the name of Jesus Christ the Nazarene whom you crucified and whom God raised from the dead by Him this man is standing here before you healthy. This is Jesus, the stone rejected by you builders, which has become the cornerstone. There is salvation in no one else, for there is no other name under heaven given to people, and we must be saved by it."
>
> —Acts 4:8-12, HCSB

What boldness! What courage! What power! The passage goes on to say that Peter's response and boldness amazed the religious rulers. After warning Peter and John not to teach about Jesus, they let them go free. This story is an example of the power and boldness that comes when someone is filled with the Holy Spirit.

Some might argue that Peter hadn't yet received the Holy Spirit at the time of his earlier denial but now has in this story, which is why he now shows such boldness. If that were the case, then every believer would demonstrate such boldness since all believers are "sealed with the promise of the Holy Spirit" (Ephesians 1:13). The Acts 4 passage makes clear that Peter's supernatural transformation was not the result of just having the Holy Spirit dwelling within. In verse 8, we see that "Peter was **filled** with the Holy Spirit."

After Peter and John were set free, they returned to their faith community to tell them about what happened. After hearing their story, the gathered believers also prayed for boldness. And the Holy Spirit answered in power.

> And when they had prayed, the place in which they were gathered together was shaken, and they were all filled with the Holy Spirit and continued to speak the word of God with boldness.
>
> —Acts 4:31

These were believers who had previously lacked power and boldness in their lives. Once they received a filling of the Holy Spirit, they were transformed into courageous witnesses for God's kingdom. What this passage makes clear is that having the Holy Spirit dwell within us and being full of the Holy Spirit are two entirely different experiences.

This Is the Normal

In so many of our lives and churches, there is an obvious lack of power and boldness. In consequence, when we encounter a group of believers full of the Holy Spirit, we may be tempted to think we are seeing something unique. But this is actually how it should be. This is the normal for God's followers. The Spirit-filled life may be unfamiliar and rarely seen for many believers, but that isn't how God wants it to be. American Christian author and pastor A. W. Tozer in his book *How to Be Filled With the Holy Spirit* phrased it this way:

> In a world where everybody was sick, health would be unusual, but it wouldn't be abnormal.
>
> —A.W. Tozer

Due to abuses and misunderstandings within the church, some factions of Christ's body have become weary and even suspicious of demonstrations of power from the Holy Spirit. This was the case even in Paul's day. That was why he encouraged the Corinthian church, which was struggling with disorderly worship services:

> So, my brothers, earnestly desire to prophesy, and do not forbid speaking in tongues. But all things should be done decently and in order.
>
> —1 Corinthians 14:39-40

The context of Paul's admonition was that the gifts of prophecy and tongues were being practiced in a chaotic, disruptive manner during worship gatherings of the Corinthian church. Since these two spiritual gifts were seen as linked closely with the manifestation of the Holy Spirit, church leadership began seeing the Holy Spirit as the one responsible for their disorderly services. Paul made clear that the real issue was a lack of structure and discernment. The solution isn't to forbid manifestations and presence of the Holy Spirit. The solution is for those practicing their gifts to do so in an orderly way that edifies the church body instead of bringing chaos and disunity.

Many churches today still get extremely nervous about where powerful demonstrations of the Holy Spirit could lead. Such churches may acknowledge doctrinally that the Holy Spirit is part of the Trinity without expecting or encouraging his interaction in their midst. The apostle Paul reminded the church in Thessalonica:

> Don't stifle the Spirit. Don't despise prophecies, but test all things. Hold
> on to what is good.
>
> —1 Thessalonians 5:19-21, HCSB

But in a desire for order and/or fear of losing control, too many churches forbid anything that can't be scheduled or planned for in their gatherings. As a consequence, too many spiritual leaders have learned to ignore the person of the Holy Spirit and have gotten good at doing church without him. Sadly, in the process they've also given up the power and boldness they could have in their lives, ministries, and congregations. As Paul reminded a fearful Timothy, God did not give us a spirit of fear but a Spirit of Power!

REFLECT AND APPLY

What would be some possible outcomes of receiving the fullness of God's Spirit in your life?

CHAPTER ELEVEN

RECEIVING THE FULLNESS OF GOD'S SPIRIT

For God gave us a spirit not of fear but of power . . .

—2 Timothy 1:7

And don't get drunk with wine, which leads to reckless actions but be filled by the Spirit.

—Ephesians 5:18 (HCSB)

Are you a disciple of Jesus who desires to live for his kingdom but still struggles with a spirit of fear that is holding you back from walking in obedience to God? Do you lack power in your ministry or boldness in your witness? If the answer to either question is yes, then ask the Father for a fresh filling of the Holy Spirit along with the resolve to fully surrender to his will. The apostle Paul reminds:

> For it is God who works in you, both to will and to work for his good pleasure.
>
> —Philippians 2:13

As a follower of Christ, God has already given you his Spirit. But it is also his desire to give the Holy Spirit to you in increasing measure as you "work out your own salvation with fear and trembling (Philippians 2:12b)."

Interacting with a Person of the Godhead

When you ask for the Father's greatest gift, be careful to examine your motivations for wanting more of the Holy Spirit. Do you desire his power in order to enhance his kingdom or your own? Are you truly interested in knowing the third Person of the Godhead, or is it that you want others to know of you? You may long to have a greater filling of God's Spirit and power, but to what end?

There is no specific method that will guarantee you spiritual power. But there are biblical principles that will help you interact with a Person of the Godhead. And as you develop a relationship with the Holy Spirit, you will see an increase of power and boldness in your life.

PRINCIPLE #1: KEEP ASKING, SEARCHING, AND KNOCKING

Among the parables Jesus told is one about a persistent man who keeps knocking on his neighbor's door until he gets what he came for (Luke 11:5-8). I can picture this scenario vividly because my wife and I lived our own version of it while ministering in a remote East African village. Among local customs was giving a verbal "knock" when you visited a home. This meant literally calling out "knock, knock" in the local language when you arrived at someone's door.

We would get these verbal knocks at all hours day and night. Sometimes to borrow a tool. Sometimes because a pregnant woman needed to be driven to the hospital. There were many days when my wife and I felt we had nothing left to give. We would occasionally even stay very quiet and out of sight of the windows, pretending we weren't home (we may have been missionaries, but we were also very human!). Usually the person at the door would verbally knock for an inhuman length of time without giving up. Sometimes they'd take a break, and we'd think they were gone, only to discover they were just resting before their next knocking session.

More often than not, we eventually caved in and answered the door. I can assure you, this wasn't because they were our neighbor but because we knew we'd have to continue putting up with this verbal knocking until we dealt with it. This type of everyday scenario is what Jesus's audience would have visualized when they heard his parable about the persistent neighbor. Jesus finished his story with the following application.

> And I tell you, ask, and it will be given to you; seek, and you will find; knock, and it will be opened to you. For everyone who asks receives, and the one who seeks finds, and to the one who knocks it will be opened.
>
> —Luke 11:9-10

There is a point to this parable (and my own story). While people don't typically enjoy being pestered by their neighbors, God is always waiting for us to knock on his door. As we knock on God's door, we need to be persistent in asking for his Spirit until our Father gives him to us (for the first time and then in increasing measure). God desires that we have a long-term commitment to our relationship with the Holy Spirit and not just a one-time prayer. Yes, it starts with a first prayer, and God honors this beginning effort. But as we continue to pursue the Holy Spirit, our relationship with him grows deeper as does his presence and power in our lives.

PRINCIPLE #2: TRUST THAT THE FATHER WILL DO AS JESUS SAID, BUT DON'T DICTATE HOW

Our job is not only to keep on asking, seeking, and knocking but also to expect that God will answer. It's the Father's job to send his Spirit. In fact, Jesus finished the above parable about the persistent neighbor by telling his listeners that God as the ultimate good Father will give the Holy Spirit to all those who ask.

> If you then, who are evil, know how to give good gifts to your children, how much more will the heavenly Father give the Holy Spirit to those who ask him!
>
> —Luke 11:13

This isn't a maybe or a hopefully, but a flat-out statement of fact. And if God says it, he will do it.

> God is not human, that he should lie, not a human being, that he should change his mind. Does he speak and then not act? Does he promise and not fulfill?
>
> —Numbers 23:19, NIV

The problem is that we have certain prejudices and expectations depending on our theology, denomination, or experiences on just how God will send his Spirit. In the Greek and Hebrew languages, the word for **wind** and **spirit** are the same. When speaking to Nicodemus, Jesus used this play of words to highlight the point that you can't predict the comings and goings of the Holy Spirit.

> The Spirit is like the wind that blows wherever it wants to. You can hear the wind, but you don't know where it comes from or where it is going.
>
> —John 3:8, CEV

What's important to remember from this verse is that the Holy Spirit is a mystery we can observe but can't predict. So when you come earnestly to the Father to ask for his best gift, you can fully expect that God will give you his Spirit. But when the Holy Spirit comes, he may manifest himself in many different situations and ways. Below are just a few we see in Scripture.

- He may land on you like a peaceful dove as he did during Jesus's baptism (Matthew 3:16).
- He may bubble up inside you like a spring of living water as he did with the woman at the well (John 4:14).
- He may fall on you in tongues of holy fire as he did with the early church (Acts 2:3-4).
- He may blow through you like a wind as Jesus explained to Nicodemus (John 3:8).

Whatever manner in which the Holy Spirit manifests, it is his choice how he reveals himself to us. We need to be content with his presence rather than demanding that he arrive in some preconceived fashion.

Principle #3: Work with and not against the Holy Spirit

The entire fourth chapter of Paul's epistle to the Ephesian church talks about how we are able to live our new life in Christ by working with the Holy Spirit and not against him. It also helps us understand what it means practically to be filled with the Spirit as a lifestyle. We won't be looking at the entire chapter here, but the following segment gives us the key.

> To put off your old self, which belongs to your former manner of life and is corrupt through deceitful desires, and to be renewed in the spirit of your minds, and to put on the new self, created after the likeness of God in true righteousness and holiness.
>
> —Ephesians 4:22-24

Notice that this Spirit-filled lifestyle is centered around the concept of putting off our old corrupt, deceitful self and putting on our new holy self that is "the likeness of God" in the same sense that we were originally created in God's image (Genesis 1:26). The passage includes both active and passive elements. We are to actively do the work of putting off sin in our lives, but we are also passively being renewed by the Holy Spirit. It is easy to focus on one of these elements to the neglect of the other, but both are essential and together create a synergy.

The Holy Spirit desires to fill us with his presence and make us more like Christ. But we can work against his desires, which will hinder this process of renewal. This is why we are warned in Ephesians 4:30 not to "grieve the Holy Spirit of God" by refusing to submit to his work in our lives.

When we learn to work with and not against the Holy Spirit, we will experience what it means to be filled by him. This filling will happen repeatedly and with an increasing measure in our lives. We see a great example of this truth in the apostle Paul's admonition to the Ephesian church.

And don't get drunk with wine, which leads to reckless actions but be filled by the Spirit.

—Ephesians 5:18, HCSB

This verse warns us about the pitfalls of drunkenness, but its key point is to compare the process of getting drunk to being filled with the Holy Spirit. The more we drink of the Holy Spirit, the more our personalities and lives will be taken over by his influence. This begs a question of us. When it comes to the Holy Spirit, are we "social drinkers" who may partake once or twice a week when we get together with others, or is drinking a lifestyle for us?

If your practice is to drink alcohol all day every day, then you're in trouble. But if you are continually getting intoxicated with the Holy Spirit, the exact opposite will be true. You will soon leave the old flesh behind and instead will experience a new life in abundance.

REFLECT AND APPLY

What in this chapter did you disagree with theologically or were uncomfortable with personally? Take time to pray through these areas and dig into the Scriptures, allowing God to bring his discernment and clarity to them.

CHAPTER TWELVE

THE PARADOX OF FEAR AND LOVE

For God gave us a spirit not of fear but of power and love . . .

—2 Timothy 1:7

Let no one despise you for your youth, but set the believers an example in speech, in conduct, in love, in faith, in purity. Until I come, devote yourself to the public reading of Scripture, to exhortation, to teaching. Do not neglect the gift you have . . .

—1 Timothy 4:12-14a

LIVING FROM A PLACE OF LOVE CAN OFTEN GET very complicated as we interact with others in this fallen world. Timothy was very aware of this fact when he found himself assigned to warn certain people in the Ephesian church "not to teach any different doctrine" than the gospel Paul had preached to them (1 Timothy 1:3). While we don't know just how old Timothy was at the time of this ministry posting, Bible commentators have speculated possibly in his twenties or even somewhat older. Paul's encouragement not to let others despise Timothy for his youth and his exhortation to treat older church members as a father or mother indicates Timothy must have been significantly younger than some of these false teachers he'd been given the responsibility to confront.

PUTTING FEARS ASIDE AND EMBRACING SACRIFICIAL LOVE

Timothy would naturally have been nervous about how these older, more established church members might respond to his charges against them. But if left unchecked, this spirit of fear had the potential to hold Timothy back from ministering to the very people to whom God had called him. This was why Paul urged Timothy to set aside his spirit of fear and embrace the Spirit of love (2 Timothy 1:7).

Choosing to embrace the Spirit of love instead of the spirit of fear in this situation would give Timothy the freedom to ask just how he could best foster his congregation's relationship with God. It would also challenge him to think about what was good for the church body over what was comfortable for him. It would encourage Timothy to go to those teaching false doctrine in truth but also with a humble heart. And love would remind him that it was his calling to serve the very people trying to sideline him. We know this because love in the Person of Jesus Christ did just that.

THE LOVE/FEAR CONNECTION

For much of my life, I was so preoccupied with **not having a spirit of fear** that I completely missed the heart of 2 Timothy 1:7, which is **having the Spirit of love**. That was a tragedy because without love, any power I might have in ministry amounts to absolutely nothing. Zero gain. All loss. God finds his gifted but loveless servants utterly annoying. Why? Like fingernails on an old slate chalkboard, they may grab people's attention, but there is no blessing or edification in it, only a desire to seek personal attention. That is what the apostle Paul meant when he wrote:

> If I speak in the tongues of men and of angels, but have not love, I am a noisy gong or a clanging cymbal. And if I have prophetic powers, and understand all mysteries and all knowledge, and if I have all faith, so as to remove mountains, but have not love, I am nothing. If I give away all I have, and if I deliver up my body to be burned, but have not love, I gain nothing.
>
> —1 Corinthians 13:1-3

Another hang-up I had with the entire spirit of fear vs. spirit of love concept was that I just didn't see a connection between love and fear. If you'd asked me what the opposite of love was, I would have responded with hate. Upon further reflection, I might have added indifference. But the more I explored Paul's statement to Timothy and other related passages, the more I recognized that the antithesis of love is not hate but fear. In fact, the apostle John made this very statement in one of his own epistles.

> There is no fear in love, but perfect love casts out fear. For fear has to do with punishment, and whoever fears has not been perfected in love.
>
> —1 John 4:18

That makes sense because the driving force behind the choices we make usually stems from either love or fear. I came to this conclusion after keeping a journal for a couple days on the choices I was making. My goal was to record as many of the decisions I made throughout the day that I could remember. Along with this, I would try to analyze why I made these decisions the way I did. What was the motivating emotion behind them? Did I make them out of love for God and/or others? Or were they made from a place of personal fear?

Here are two entries from my journal in which I wrestle through the emotions of love and fear while making different choices throughout my day.

ENTRY #1:

One minor situation where I had to choose between fear and love happened while picking out what clothes to wear this morning. As I write this, my wife and I are coming to the end of our first year living in the Middle East.

A milestone worth celebrating. But today we had an even bigger reason to celebrate: our seven-year anniversary. To mark this occasion, we had a long day of activities planned, which included going to a pottery café to paint. While preparing for our time out, I noticed that my wife was pretty dressed up and looking beautiful. My mind immediately went to the fact that we'd be painting. I didn't want to wear anything too nice I might mess up. My wife, however, had it in her mind that this would be a romantic day and should include a little dressing up. I had a choice to make. I could let the fear of ruining a nice outfit squash my wife's enthusiasm, or I could say, "It's just clothes." Even if I splashed paint all over my nice khakis, it wasn't the end of the world. I went with the loving choice. I'm glad I didn't go with my gut reaction of fear because we ended up having a fun day of café and bookstore hopping and never got around to painting at the pottery café. More importantly, I think my wife felt the day was a little more special for having dressed up.

Entry #2:

A slightly more intense moment of fear and love happened today as we left our favorite local bakery carrying a bag of baked goods to enjoy at a nearby coffee shop. Walking down the street, we passed what appeared to be a down-and-out mom camped out on the sidewalk with her two children. A tug at my heart was quickly followed by fear as a flood of questions entered my mind. Was this just a ploy? Was she a professional beggar? Was she being pimped out by someone? Were those kids even hers? I'd been warned about all of these possibilities when I first arrived in this city. Then I heard the Holy Spirit whisper to me, "How would Christ with his perfect love handle this situation?" At the very least, he'd engage the woman instead of scurrying past. Actually looking at the woman for the first time, I noticed she was selling tissues. "Selling" a low-valued product everyone needs is an acceptable way in the Middle East for the down-and-out to make some money. It allowed the woman to keep her dignity even as I willingly paid more than her asking price so I could help her out. Had I allowed fear to rule the day, my wife and I would have missed out on the opportunity to love this woman and her children in a very practical and appropriate manner.

I don't mention these stories to pat myself on the back since my initial reaction in both situations came from a place of fear. I include them as examples of how often we make decisions without even realizing it as a reaction to certain fears in our lives. If we can acknowledge this and intentionally make our decisions from a spirit of love, the outcomes will be drastically different and in very positive ways.

REFLECT AND APPLY

Commit to journaling about all the decisions you make for the next two to three days. In your entries, make sure to analyze what emotions your decisions are coming from. Finally, record any new insights you gained through this experience.

Chapter Thirteen
God's Love Poured Into Us

Anyone who does not love does not know God, because God is love.

—1 John 4:8

God's love has been poured into our hearts through the Holy Spirit who has been given to us. For while we were still weak, at the right time Christ died for the ungodly. For one will scarcely die for a righteous person—though perhaps for a good person one would dare even to die— but God shows his love for us in that while we were still sinners, Christ died for us. Since, therefore, we have now been justified by his blood, much more shall we be saved by him from the wrath of God.

—Romans 5:5b-9

WHEN WE SPEAK OF GOD AS LOVE, it's important to understand what that means. When 1 John 4:8 says that "God is love," it is not saying that "love is god." Many songs, movies, and social media platforms of our day elevate love as an end to itself. By doing this, they make it a god and become idolaters. On the other extreme, there are those who only see love as one of God's many attributes. This is also a mistake as it misses the very core of God's character. Love isn't just a part of who God is but by definition his very nature.

DEFINING LOVE—GOD THE FATHER

In 2 Timothy 1:7, Paul tells Timothy that as believers we've been given a Spirit of love. This Spirit is one that flows from the very essence of the "God of love" (1 Corinthians 13:4-7). We may come to God with love for him in our hearts, but that love has not yet reached perfection because it is only a reasonable reaction to the lavish love God himself pours out on us.

> In this is love, not that we have loved God but that he loved us and sent his Son to be the propitiation for our sins.
>
> —1 John 4:10

We were all enemies of God, steeped in our sin and rebellion. Yet God still pursued us at significant cost to himself. God had nothing to gain by loving us. In fact, bringing us back into a loving relationship with God cost him the life of his only Son. If God had nothing to gain and everything to lose by loving us, then why did he do it? He did it because that is who he is. God is love.

DEMONSTRATING LOVE—GOD THE SON

Jesus set the ultimate example of love when he died on the cross in our place. Giving one's life for another person is a rare sacrifice few individuals would consider making. In his epistle to the Romans, the apostle Paul recognizes that while someone might perhaps be willing to die for a good person, before Christ we had no chance of fitting into this category. But though we were morally hopeless and ungodly, Christ died for us, saving us from God's wrath.

> For while we were still weak, at the right time Christ died for the ungodly. For one will scarcely die for a righteous person—though perhaps for a good person one would dare even to die—but God shows his love for us in that while we were still sinners, Christ died for us. Since, therefore, we have now been justified by his blood, much more shall we be saved by him from the wrath of God.
>
> —Romans 5:6-9

To truly grasp how great an act of love this was, one needs to fully understand the concept of propitiation as mentioned above in 1 John 4:10. Propitiation means satisfaction. When we use the term theologically, it refers to how God was able to provide us with salvation and yet still have his justice (wrath) satisfied. In summary, God is saying, "If I punish mankind for their sin, they will all die and go to hell. On the other hand, if I don't punish mankind for their sin, my justice will never be satisfied."

How did God solve this propitiation problem? He satisfied his divine requirement for justice by laying it on Jesus, who made the payment for our sin through his death on the cross. The second verse of Irish American hymn writer Charlie Lee Smith's *Before the Throne of God Above*, gives a beautiful description of Christ's demonstration of love to us—propitiation.

> When Satan tempts me to despair
> And tells me of the guilt within
> Upward I look, and see Him there
> who made an end to all my sin
>
> Because the sinless Savior died
> My sinful soul is counted free
> For God the just is satisfied
> To look on Him and pardon me
> To look on Him and pardon me

DISTRIBUTING LOVE—GOD THE HOLY SPIRIT

God the Father's extravagant love demonstrated through the sacrifice of his Son Jesus Christ is poured into our hearts when we place our faith in him through the deposit of the Holy Spirit, who is the distributor of God's gifts:

And hope does not put us to shame, because God's love has been poured out into our hearts through the Holy Spirit, who has been given to us.

—Romans 5:5

When you believed, you were marked in him [Christ] with a seal, the promised Holy Spirit, who is a deposit guaranteeing our inheritance.

—Ephesians 1:13-14a, NIV

The presence of God's abundant love in us is evidence of being his child and the eternal hope all believers can stand on in life or death, a hope that "does not put us to shame" (Romans 5:5). We have this hope as believers because "we have been justified by faith" (Romans 5:5) and "we have peace with God" (Romans 5:1). Therefore, we have no reason to fear what will happen on the final Day of Judgment as the apostle John reminds:

For fear has to do with punishment, and whoever fears has not been perfected in love.

—1 John 4:18b

What we see in the above verse is that, even though God pours his love into us through his Spirit at the time of our salvation, there is still a process of maturing in that love. This perfecting process happens as we remain rooted and grounded in the Father's love because his Spirit also remains in us to help us understand the true magnitude of that love.

That according to the riches of his glory he may grant you to be strengthened with power through his Spirit in your inner being, so that Christ may dwell in your hearts through faith—that **you, being rooted**

111

and grounded in love, **may have strength to comprehend with all the saints what is the breadth and length and height and depth, and to know the love of Christ that surpasses knowledge,** that you may be filled with all the fullness of God. (emphasis mine)

—Ephesians 3:16-19

Through the Holy Spirit's presence and the enlightenment he brings, the fear in our hearts is increasingly replaced with God's love to the point that our understanding of God's love is beyond mere intellectual knowledge because our souls have experienced his love in ways that transcend the ability of our minds to understand. We have now reached perfection in love (1 John 4:18) and are "filled with all the fullness of God" (Ephesians 19).

REFLECT AND APPLY

Since the time of your salvation, how have your experiences of God's love matured your love and brought you into a deeper fullness of God?

GOING DEEPER

SUGGESTED ACTIVITIES

1. Research what the "spiritual greats" of the past believed about the Holy Spirit. Allow them to lead you on a journey of exploration with the goal of experiencing the Third Person of the Godhead in a way that surpasses all understanding.

2. Keep a love/fear journal for two to three days (explained in chapter twelve page 101).

SUGGESTED READING:

Top 7 Classics on the Holy Spirit by Torrey, Murray, Simpson, Brengle, Edwards, Campbell, Gordon.

Forgotten God by Francis Chan.

Powerlines: What Great Evangelicals Believed about the Holy Spirit 1850-1930 , Leona Frances Choy.

SECTION FOUR:
CULTIVATING THE
RIGHT MINDSET

God, my Father, may your word dwell richly
In my heart from hour to hour,
So that all may see I triumph
Only through your power.
Christ, my Savior, may your mind
Live in me from day to day,
By your love and power controlling
All I do and say.
Holy Spirit, my comforter, may your peace
Rule my life in everything
That I may be calm to console
The sick and sorrowing.

—adapted from *May the Mind of Christ My Savior*
by Kate B. Wilkinson,
Keswick Convention Movement, 1913

CHAPTER FOURTEEN
CULTIVATING A MINDSET OF JOY

For God has not given us a spirit of fear, but of power and of love and of a sound mind.

—2 Timothy 1:7, NIV

For me to live is Christ and to die is gain.

—Philippians 1:21

Let this mind be in you which was also in Christ Jesus.

—Philippians 2:5, BSB

ANCIENT GREEK PHILOSOPHER THALES OF MILETUS stated, "The most difficult thing in life is to know yourself."

While a true statement, I think it is also indicative of the reality that Thales remained a lifelong bachelor. There is nothing quite like the commitment of marriage to bring all our broken bits to the surface. At least that is what being in a constant intimate relationship has done in my own life. It took only a few years of marriage for me to recognize I was an angry, anxious man stuck in a loop of toxic thinking. That was when my wife and I went to a marriage counselor and I started down the long road of renewing my mind.

Years later, I am still on this journey. But I'm seeing daily victories as I allow the Holy Spirit and God's Word to reprogram the way I think and see life. I now realize that having a sound mind is more than some unrealistic ideal to chase after. It is something God wants me to have. And God has given me and every other believer all the necessary resources to develop one.

HAVING A SOUND MIND IS A COMMON STRUGGLE

I know I'm not alone in my struggle to have a sound mind. Our genetics, upbringing, and life experiences all contribute to this challenge. Nor do I believe for one minute that just because we love God, we're immune to mental health struggles. When we buy into that lie, it only heaps guilt on top of an already complex situation. Job, Hannah, and King David are just a few examples of people in the Bible who loved God dearly but had times when they struggled with anxieties and depression.

Charles Wesley, the brother of John Wesley, was a preacher God used mightily within the nineteenth century Methodist revival movement. You may recognize him as the writer of such great classic hymns as "Hark the Herald Angels Sing" and "Christ the Lord is Risen Today." But he also struggled with anxiety and depression. In his recently decrypted diary, we can read about Charles's mental health struggles brought on by his demanding ministry schedule, wife's miscarriage, and disputes with his brother.[1] Anxiety and depression were common conditions for believers in Charles Wesley's day just as they are in ours. That is why Charles's brother John addressed these "nervous disorders" in many sermons and letters.

THE SOPHRONISMOS MIND

A strong case could be made that Timothy also dealt with social anxieties and the stomach issues that often come with them (1 Timothy 5:23). This was a very understandable condition for a young man serving a congregation that didn't respect his leadership. But in Paul's letters to Timothy, the apostle reminds this youthful church leader that his anxieties do not come from God. Rather, the Holy Spirit, who does come from God, brings order to the chaos in our heads and enables us to have a "sound mind."

The Greek word translated as "sound mind" in this verse is *sophronismos*, which refers to a disciplined mind under the control of God's

Spirit. The word is translated in other English versions as self-control, self-restraint, and sound or good judgment.

We can describe the *sophronismos* mind as one that is full of joy, peace, and order. Having a healthy mind like this requires a thought process based on the wisdom and insights the Holy Spirit gives rather than the noise in our heads or the propaganda of the world, both of which manipulate us through fear. This is the mind Paul wanted Timothy to have. The mind Paul knew Timothy could have through the Holy Spirit.

Being Christ-Focused Cultivates a Joyful Mindset

Paul doesn't expound any further on the *sophronismos* mind in his letter to Timothy. However, he does address it in his epistle to the Philippians, which Timothy helped him write (Philippians 1:1), a letter filled with practical insights on how to have a mind full of joy, peace, and order. How does this happen? The apostle Paul makes clear that it comes through cultivating a Christ-like mindset.

> In your relationships with one another, **have the same mindset as Christ Jesus.** (emphasis mine)
>
> —Philippians 2:5, NIV

When I think about situations that threaten to steal my joyful mindset, it's not the demise of my ministry or possibility of being executed but everyday things like not getting food into my belly fast enough when I'm hungry. In contrast, when Paul wrote his letter to the Philippians, he had some very legitimate challenges threatening to steal his joy if he let them.

For starters, he was under twenty-four hour house arrest for two long years (Acts 28:30-31). A go-getter with boundless energy, Paul was used to traveling the known world in order to preach the gospel of Christ. Suddenly, all this was taken away, and he found himself restricted to one location with guards watching his every move. If that wasn't bad enough, there were other so-called Christian teachers trying to sabotage his ministry, preaching Christi:

> ... from envy and rivalry . . . out of selfish ambition, not sincerely but thinking to afflict me in my imprisonment.
>
> —Philippians 1:15-18

These people were not lovingly filling in for Paul because of his imprisonment but were trying to take over his ministry when they knew he could do nothing about it. Then came Paul's most serious challenge as he awaited trial by Caesar. This situation was made even more precarious because the ruling Caesar at this time was Nero, a twisted soul who used Christians as human torches to illuminate his gardens at night. So Paul was well aware of the unlikelihood that he would walk away with his life.

Yet in the midst of all of this, we find Paul full of joy. What is his secret? It's his perspective. He filters everything that comes into his life through one thought.

> For me to live is Christ and to die is gain.
>
> —Philippians 1:21

Paul's single-minded obsession with doing whatever would bring Christ the most glory allowed him to experience life in a way few people ever will. Most of us view life through the lens of our circumstances. When we do this, we place ourselves in a passive role that makes us the victim of life's hardships. This perspective is devoid of power and joy and will end in toxic thinking about ourselves, others, and God.

But when we see life through the perspective of using every situation to bring glory to Christ, then life can only be full of opportunities. Paul understood that while happiness may depend on what happens to us, joy comes from having the right perspective.

Keeping this "Christ glorified" perspective in mind, let's revisit the challenges in Paul's life. He was under house arrest and being watched by Roman guards twenty-four hours a day. These guards, who rotated every four hours, would have been chained to Paul while he prayed, talked with other believers, and wrote epistles to the early churches. Instead of seeing this as an intrusion, Paul viewed being chained to these men as divine appointments to share Christ with a captive audience.

> Now I want you to know, brothers and sisters, that what has happened to me has actually served to advance the gospel. As a result, it has become clear throughout the whole palace guard and to everyone else that I am in chains for Christ.
>
> —Philippians 1:12-13, NIV

Paul's second challenge came from the very "preachers of the gospel" who should have come alongside him in his time of need but were instead taking advantage of his helpless state. How does Paul handle this betrayal? Again, he looks at it through the perspective of a Christ-focused mindset, rejoicing that Christ is being preached, regardless of motives.

> But what does it matter? The important thing is that in every way, whether from false motives or true, Christ is preached. And because of this I rejoice.
>
> —Philippians 1:18, NIV

A final challenge Paul faced here was the reality that he could very likely lose his life for the gospel. In moments when our mortality is threatened, we see what really lies within our hearts. When Satan was tormenting Job, his last and final test was to ruin his health. He said to God, "Let me take away his health and he will curse you" (Job 2:5). With all of human history to draw from, Satan knew that people usually see life through the perspective of self-preservation.

Satan was surprised to find that this was not the case with Job. I imagine he was equally amazed at Paul's response (my own paraphrase): "If I live, it will be to honor Christ with my life, and if I die, I will try to glorify Christ with my death" (Philippians 1:21).

Whatever would bring the most glory to Christ was a win for Paul. A perspective like this can only come through a single-minded focus on Christ and desire to see him glorified.[2]

BEING OTHERS-FOCUSED CULTIVATES A JOYFUL MINDSET

Having a single-minded focus on Christ will lead us to having the mind of Christ. This is a natural progression since as the nineteenth-century poet

William Blake once wrote: "We become what we behold." So let's prayerfully behold Christ Jesus as the apostle Paul described him in his epistle to the Philippians.

> Have this mind among yourselves, which is yours in Christ Jesus, who, though he was in the form of God, did not count equality with God a thing to be grasped, but emptied himself, by taking the form of a servant, being born in the likeness of men. And being found in human form, he humbled himself by becoming obedient to the point of death, even death on a cross. Therefore God has highly exalted him and bestowed on him the name that is above every name, so that at the name of Jesus every knee should bow, in heaven and on earth and under the earth, and every tongue confess that Jesus Christ is Lord, to the glory of God the Father.
>
> —Philippians 2:5-11

In this passage, we see that Christ has a mind that is humble and others-focused. Earlier in this same chapter, Paul tells us to have that same others-focused mind.

> Do nothing from selfish ambition or conceit, but in humility count others more significant than yourselves. Let each of you look not only to his own interests, but also to the interests of others.
>
> —Philippians 2:3-4

The first step in becoming others-focused is to make sure we guard against rivalry and conceit, both of which are self-focused. Rivalry focuses on elevating ourselves because we feel we are worth less than others. Conceit focuses on elevating ourselves because we believe we are worth more than others. The irony is that in both situations, being self-focused does the exact opposite of what we are striving for. Instead of lifting us up and enhancing our lives, it pulls us down into anxiety and depression.

Instead of these self-focused perspectives, we should consider "others better than ourselves" (v. 3). This can only be done through genuine humility and self-forgetfulness. It is perfectly normal to think about yourself as you take care of your needs and responsibilities. That's what healthy adults do. The problem is when you focus on yourself at the expense of others in your life.

We default to this way of thinking because we intuitively feel that in order for us to go up, others have to go down. But Jesus knew that the exact opposite was true. He understood that when we go down to lift others up, we actually all go up together. He deliberately went down below others so that he might lift them up. Because of this attitude, not only was he able to lift us out of our sin and shame but "God [also] highly exalted him and bestowed on him the name that is above every name" (v. 9).

REFLECT AND APPLY

Happiness depends on happenings, but joy depends on perspective. What situations in your life are causing you unhappiness? How can you view them through a perspective of joy?

CHAPTER FIFTEEN
CULTIVATING A MINDSET OF PEACE

For God has not given us a spirit of fear, but of power and of love and of a sound mind.

—2 Timothy 1:7, NIV

Do not be anxious about anything, but in everything by prayer and supplication with thanksgiving let your requests be known to God. And the peace of God, which surpasses all understanding will guard your hearts and minds in Christ Jesus.

—Philippians 4:6-7

ACCORDING TO PHILIPPIANS 4:6-7, we have two choices in life. We can be anxious people, or we can go to God and receive a peace only he can give. When we are offered such an easy decision, why do we so often feel compelled to worry rather than choose to have peace?

The simple answer is that on some level we all want to control the circumstances that affect our lives. The problem is that there is very little in this world we can control. To admit this flies in the face of the American dream, the self-help movement, and the prosperity gospel. Yet it's a reality we must face if we ever want to move past being anxious people. Nick Wigmill, clinical psychologist and author in his article "Why We Worry (and How to Stop),"[1] sums up this dilemma well.

> We may not be able to actually do anything about a problem, but worrying about it makes us feel like we're doing something.
>
> —Nick Wigmill

Busying ourselves with frantic thought somehow sits better with us than dwelling on the fact that we are unable to control the outcome of a situation. At least it sits well initially. But eventually worrying turns us into anxious people, and it ruins our minds and bodies. Many of our sleepless nights, sour stomachs, and pounding heads come from our unwillingness to let go of the illusion of control.

SURRENDERING CONTROL IN PRAYER BRINGS GOD'S PEACE

In Philippians 4:6-7 (see above), Paul warns us not to be seduced by the momentary allures of worry. Instead of channeling our nervous energy inward, which leads to anxiety, we are to direct it upward in prayer, which leads to God's peace. Paul instructs us in these verses to pray in a general sense but also encourages us to come to God with supplications. Under the guidance of the Holy Spirit, Paul has given us written permission to walk into God's throne room and lay our needs at God's feet. This can be a little intimidating when we consider the galaxies God spoke into existence, and it is easy to wonder with King David:

> When I look at your heavens, the work of your fingers, the moon and the stars, which you have set in place, what is man that you are mindful of him, and the son of man that you care for him?
>
> —Psalm 8:3-4

But as much of a mystery as this may be, the wonderful truth remains that the God of the universe is also our heavenly Father, and he cares for us deeply. That is why we can make our supplications to God with thanksgiving. It's not so much that we are thankful for the needy situation in which we find ourselves, although there is a place for being grateful in all circumstances, but that God sees our needs, cares about us, and will act on our behalf. Jesus himself promised as much in his teachings on fear and anxiety.

> Look at the birds of the air: they neither sow nor reap nor gather into barns, and yet your heavenly Father feeds them. Are you not of more value than they?
>
> —Matthew 6:26

> Are not two sparrows sold for a penny? And not one of them will fall to
> the ground apart from your Father.
>
> —Matthew 10:29

At the time Jesus spoke these words, the Roman penny, or *assarion*, was enough to buy a loaf of bread—or two sparrows. The bottom line is that sparrows weren't considered worth much, at least in the marketplace. But God, who took the time to create them, finds them so valuable that he feeds them and doesn't let one of them fall to the ground dead without noticing and caring. If this is how God feels about such an "insignificant" creature, how much more value does he place on us as his dearly loved children?

When we take Jesus at his word, trusting that our heavenly Father highly values us and promises to meet all of our needs, we can rest in God's providence and receive his peace. This process will involve bringing our needs to him with a humility that admits we are helpless both in our knowledge of what is best and in our ability to make it happen.

Living in Obedience to God Brings His Peace

While I find a lot of spiritual platitudes in the bumper sticker genre rather trite, I appreciate the oldie but goodie that reads: "No God, No Peace. Know God, Know Peace." The apostle Paul takes this thought one step further when he goes on to say in his letter to the Philippians that obedience to God is the means by which we know him and receive his peace.

> What you have learned and received and heard and seen in me—practice
> these things and the God of peace will be with you.
>
> —Philippians 4:9

In other words, when we live in obedience to God, the God of obedience will be with us. This isn't a call to legalism, which mandates perfect adherence to God's rules before he will consider drawing near to us. Instead, this is a heart attitude that desires to obey God in all things because we love him. When we make up our minds to not only hear God's Word but also seek its application in our lives, then God finds in us a welcoming dwelling place in which he can fully abide. And with his presence in our home comes his peace in our lives. We can't expect to live in apathy or open rebellion against God's Word and still experience his presence and peace.

One powerful Old Testament story (Daniel 6) vividly depicts how God's peace is present in our lives when we obey God, even in the most challenging situations. The story is about a Judean exile taken to live in the ancient city-state of Babylon, which is modern day Iraq. The Babylonians called him Belteshazzar, which means "the spirit of the holy gods is in him." You may know him better from Sunday school as the prophet Daniel.

Because of God's hand on him, Daniel rose in power to become second only to the king. This didn't go over well with other local political rulers, who looked for anything they could use to bring him down. To their disappointment, they couldn't find even a hint of wrongdoing in his personal or political life. So they devised a plan to put a wedge between the king and Daniel by using Daniel's devotion to God as a trap.

Through unabashed flattery, they tricked the king into signing an irrevocable decree that for thirty days no one should make a petition or prayer to anyone but the king on penalty of being thrown into a pit full of hungry lions. When Daniel heard about the decree, he didn't hesitate to do exactly what he'd always done. With his windows opened wide, he got on his knees and prayed aloud to God (Daniel 6:10). It's as if he was trying to make a very clear statement as to whose kingdom he really belonged to and which King he would obey above all others.

The local rulers immediately reported Daniel's response to the king, who was instantly sorry he'd made this rash law. With great sorrow, the king sent Daniel to the pit of lions with this farewell: "May the God whom you serve continually rescue you" (vs. 16). That night the king couldn't eat or sleep (v. 18). Meanwhile, Daniel spent a peaceful night in the pit of lions because God's presence was with him. When the king rushed down at daybreak to find out Daniel's fate, Daniel calmly informed him that God had sent an angel to shut the lions' mouths (vv. 21-22).

Like Daniel, when we know God and walk in obedience to God's ways whatever the cost, we can have his peace regardless of how dire our situation may be. If we don't know God, then even the biggest palace with all the pleasures it may provide will not bring us lasting peace.

REFLECT AND APPLY

What situation are you trying to control in your life right now? How is that working out for you? Why have you been hesitant to go to the Father in "prayer and thanksgiving" over this issue?

CHAPTER SIXTEEN

CULTIVATING A MINDSET OF ORDER

Finally, brothers, whatever is true, whatever is honorable, whatever is just, whatever is pure, whatever is lovely, whatever is commendable, if there is any excellence, if there is anything worthy of praise, think about these things.

—Philippians 4:8

Do not be conformed to this world but be transformed by the renewal of your mind, that by testing you may discern what is the will of God, what is good and acceptable and perfect.

—Romans 12:2

AS EARLY AS TWO MONTHS AFTER CONCEPTION, we humans start to develop ears. Before we are even born, we can hear voices and distinguish between them.[1] The earliest voices come to us from our families and other caregivers. But as life unfolds, we are introduced to the voices of peers, teachers, pastors, coworkers, and spouses. If flesh and blood weren't enough, there are still more voices on the radio, TV, movies, podcasts, and social media. Hopefully amidst all the noise, there are also moments set aside to hear God's voice.

We can limit the volume and kind of voices that bombard us, which is very important, but we can't silence them altogether. And sometimes we're just not equipped to navigate the things these voices say, especially when we are young. Before we are even old enough to fully understand, life can send hurtful messages our way. From that point on, we also hear inner voices in the form of self-talk that cripple our ability to think in healthy ways.

THE VOICES TO WHICH WE LISTEN

Because of toxic voices that were part of my life growing up, I formed unhealthy thought patterns that put a lot of stress on my marriage, especially in the early years. In moments of clarity, I knew my patterns of thinking were sabotaging my marriage and affecting my mental and physical health. But I'd been walking the same beaten-down paths for so long there were ruts in the ground, and I had no idea how to change these patterns.

In this time of hopelessness, God showed me that Romans 12:2 should be taken quite literally when the apostle Paul urges: "Do not conform to the patterns of this world, but be transformed by the renewing of your mind."

Science is now confirming what the Bible has already said for thousands of years, i.e., that we can literally change our brains. Dr. Caroline Leaf, neuroscientist and author, notes in her book *Switch on Your Brain*: "Thoughts are real, physical things that occupy mental real estate."

She goes on to explain that we have the ability to strengthen or weaken our thoughts through purposeful manipulation. Scientists call this ability to manipulate the brain *neuroplasticity*. The common school of thought used to be that we hard-wire our brains in childhood and that after childhood we are incapable of changing them. More recently, scientists have discovered that we can at any stage in our lives change the way we think and perceive our world.

The challenge is that after childhood our brains stop being in a constant state of flux, so changing them takes a lot more intentionality.[2] Both our well-established thought patterns and the sheer volume of the world's messages are all working against us like a strong current. As the apostle Paul makes clear in the above verse, if we are not "renewing our minds," our brains will become "conformed" to all these messages. In other words, if we are not taking an active role in programming our brains, then over time we will passively conform to the voices surrounding us.

Conforming takes no effort. All we need to do is the same thing everyone else is doing. Absorb without question the plethora of voices that come at us every day. Be informed and amused by those voices without reflecting too much on what it all means. That's what normal people do. Normal sounds good, right?

Except that most "normal" people are walking around with chaos in their minds. Which in turn is spilling out into their lives. There's another and better way to live. A way of bringing order to all that chaos.

BRINGING ORDER TO THE CHAOS IN OUR MINDS

Romans 12:2 calls this transformation from chaos to order a renewal of the mind. Modern psychology labels this same process as Cognitive Behavior Therapy. CBT is a step-by-step method for identifying negative thinking and replacing it with a healthier voice. Our brains are wired to make pathways of thoughts in the form of neurons firing together. Depending on the situation in front of us, our brain will select the "appropriate" thought path to go down. The problem is that many of these established pathways are unhealthy, but we don't realize it because they are so well-worn that they've become automatic responses. CBT helps people identify these unhealthy pathways and then replace them with new, healthy ones.

I came to understand a lot of these truths through the ministry of Dr. Leaf, who has spent her life showing that science can work hand in hand with the Bible to set us free from our toxic thoughts. Participating in her Twenty-One-Day Brain Detox plan[3] was extremely helpful in showing me in practical terms what it means to renew my mind with intentionality. Over time, I've made some adaptations to her program that I've found beneficial.

First, every month I come before the Holy Spirit and reflectively read through Philippians 4:8 (see above). As I do this, I ask the Holy Spirit to show me what unhealthy thought he would have me work on this month. Once I've heard from him, I find a Bible passage that speaks God's truth to the lie of this unhealthy thought. I then start every day with a prayer of praise and thanksgiving, followed by a time of reflecting on this passage and asking God to transform my thoughts to become God's thoughts. During this time with God, I journal my thoughts, insights, and progress related to this month's unhealthy thought. I also ask God to make me aware when this thought comes to mind.

Throughout the course of the day as the Holy Spirit makes me aware of this unhealthy thought, I immediately say, "Stop in the name of Jesus." This breaks the power of the thought. I then quote the verse I've selected to meditate on. This replaces the negative thought with God's truth. By using this "renewing" principle of Romans 12:2, or Cognitive Behavioral Therapy in modern psychological terms, I am systematically tearing down my unhealthy thoughts and building up new healthy ones.

At the beginning of each new month, I repeat the process again. Perhaps the Holy Spirit will want to work on the same unhealthy thought as last month. Or maybe he will pick something new. He knows best and should be the one leading this process.

Any time we spend in God's Word, before God in prayer, and with other intentional believers will contribute towards the renewal of our minds. The Holy Spirit will use it all to help transform the way we think and live. But being deliberate about this process will increase the power and reach of your transformation. Working in tandem with the Holy Spirit and in a way that is known to be scientifically effective can make the difference between having lifelong struggles with unhealthy thought patterns and having a *sophronismos* mind of joy, peace, and order.

REFLECT AND APPLY

Has the Holy Spirit brought any unhealthy thought patterns to your attention that might be bringing disorder into your mind and life? How can you involve the Holy Spirit in intentionally bringing order to that chaos?

Going Deeper

Suggested Activities

1. Work on your perspective. Instead of a gratitude list that generally focuses on things that make us happy in a day, write down or share as a family things that bring you joy each day. Remember that joy involves the deeper truths of God's character and can be found in both the good and bad moments of our day.

2. Go on a walk in nature and observe how well God provides for even the most insignificant plant or creature. Then meditate on Matthew 6:25-34 and how much God must care for you and desire to provide for you. Let that truth bring peace to your anxious mind and free you to serve God's kingdom fully.

3. Complete Dr. Caroline Leaf's 21-Day Detox Plan (from the book *Switch on Your Brain*).

Suggested Reading:

Switch on Your Brain (includes 21-Day Detox Plan) by Dr. Caroline Leaf

SECTION FIVE:
SUFFERING
FOR THE GOSPEL

O Lord our God, you pour out your Holy Spirit on those you have set apart to be stewards of your mysteries. Keep your servant that I may hold the mystery of the faith in a pure conscience and with all virtue. Give me the grace given to your first martyr Stephen, that I may do the work to which I am called. By your holy and life-giving Spirit, fill me with all faith and love, power and sanctification. For you are my God, and to you we give glory, Father, Son, and Holy Spirit, now and ever, to ages of ages.

—Ordinal Liturgy of the Eastern Church

CHAPTER SEVENTEEN
TIMOTHY'S CHOICE TO EMBRACE SUFFERING

Therefore do not be ashamed of the testimony about our Lord, nor of me his prisoner, but share in suffering for the gospel by the power of God.

—2 Timothy 1:8

In summer 64 A.D., a massive fire roared through Rome, turning seventy percent of the city into a smoldering ash heap. It has been commonly claimed that Nero, then ruler of the Roman Empire, played the fiddle while he watched Rome burn. While it is more probable that he strummed a lyre, Nero's lackluster response to the crisis led many to believe he might have instigated this tragedy as an opportunity to enlarge his palatial residence. To shift negative public opinion from himself, Nero blamed the whole incident on Rome's Christian population.

Not content with rounding up a few Christians as scapegoats, Nero sought to capture, humiliate, and kill as many of them as he could find. The historian Tacitus, a young boy during these events, wrote that captured Christians were:

> . . . covered with the hides of wild beast, and worried to death by dogs, or nailed to crosses, or set fire to, and when the day waned, burned to serve for the evening lights.
>
> —Tacitus

Nero's treatment of the Christians was so horrific that many Romans callused to the gore of the arena felt compassion for them.[1] While details are clouded by time, many biblical scholars place Paul's arrest with this wave of persecution. And unlike his previous stint of being under house arrest (Acts 28), Paul now found himself in a dark, smelly underground dungeon.

During these perilous times, it only took a loose association with a Christian to find oneself nailed to a cross or turned into a living torch for Nero's gardens. And Paul was not just any Christian. Because of his leadership in the early church and previous trial in Rome, he was now a high-profile enemy of the state. As a result, even many Christians who had come to Rome from various congregations in Asia Minor had distanced themselves from him, including two specifically named as Phygellus and Hermogenes (2 Timothy 1:15). This disloyalty must have been particularly hurtful to Paul since he was their spiritual father and they owed their very salvation to the blood, sweat, and tears of his missionary journeys.

While some believers may have turned on Paul individually, including the self-serving preachers Paul mentioned, church history would suggest that many believers in Rome saw this move as a pragmatic one to protect themselves and their communities from persecution. No matter their reasons, these spiritual descendants of Paul were ashamed to align themselves with him for fear of Nero's gaze falling on them.

TIMOTHY'S CHOICE TO SUFFER WITH PAUL

There is no evidence that Timothy himself was distancing himself from Paul. But perhaps knowing that Timothy was prone to social anxieties, Paul wanted to encourage him that standing in solidarity with him and the gospel of Christ was both an honor and his duty. The New English Translation expresses this well.

> Therefore do not be ashamed of the testimony about our Lord nor of me
> his prisoner, but share in suffering for the gospel by the power of God.
>
> —2 Timothy 1:8

At the end of this second letter to Timothy, Paul asked him to suffer for the gospel in a very practical way. He wanted Timothy to visit him in Rome. This was no small request as it probably meant Timothy would have to secure passage aboard a Roman merchant ship on its way back from Alexandria. Because the winds were against these ships on their return trip to Rome, their voyages were slow and often full of danger.[2] Paul himself on his trip to Rome was shipwrecked on Malta for three months because of these troublesome winds (Acts 27-28).

Once Timothy did reach Rome, he would have to search "diligently" for the place where Paul was being imprisoned as had done another courageous believer and mutual acquaintance from the Ephesian church, Onesiphorus.

> May the Lord grant mercy to the household of Onesiphorus, for he often
> refreshed me and was not ashamed of my chains, but when he arrived in
> Rome he searched for me earnestly and found me . . . and you well know
> all the service he rendered at Ephesus.
>
> —2 Timothy 1:16-17

Once Timothy finally located Paul, he would be in even more danger than at sea as he'd now be in Nero's backyard associating with an enemy of the state. If Timothy accepted Paul's invitation, he would also be accepting his share of suffering for Paul and the gospel. While the New Testament and church history are silent as to whether Timothy ever made the journey, it is my conviction he at least tried based on Paul's own testimony of Timothy's character.

> For I have no one like him, who will be genuinely concerned for your welfare. For they all seek their own interests, not those of Jesus Christ. But you know Timothy's proven worth, how as a son with a father he has served with me in the gospel.
>
> —Philippians 2:20-22

REFLECT AND APPLY

What are your thoughts on suffering for the sake of the gospel? Do you agree or disagree that it is both the honor and duty of every believer? Think through and pray about your reasoning. Ask God to show you what he wants of you for the sake of the gospel.

CHAPTER EIGHTEEN
ACCEPTING OUR SHARE OF SUFFERING

For this gospel, I was appointed a herald, apostle, and teacher, and that is why I suffer these things.

—2 Timothy 1:11

Then Jesus told his disciples, "If anyone would come after me, let him deny himself and take up his cross and follow me.

—Matthew 16:24-25

Doing life in a broken world means that all humans will experience hardships at some point. But if we decide to become his disciple, Jesus makes clear that we are volunteering for a lifestyle of suffering. It is not coincidental that the first assignment Jesus gave his followers (see above) was to pick up the Romans' preferred instrument of execution, the cross. Only once they've embraced this object of suffering and death does he then invite them to follow in his steps. Jesus knew that if people persecuted and killed him, they would do the same to his followers.

Suffering Is the Natural Result of Boldly Following Christ

Make no mistake that living as a disciple of Christ means sharing in his suffering. Paul reminded Timothy that "all those who want to live a godly life in Christ Jesus will be persecuted" (2 Timothy 3:12). This is because God's kingdom runs upside-down and counter-culturally to this world. If we follow Christ, we will end up living in total opposition to what society is trying to accomplish. As we walk in the opposite direction of the masses, we are going to stand out. When this happens, the Bible explains in vivid language the reactions we will get from people.

Because of Christ, we give off a sweet scent rising to God, which is recognized by those on the way of salvation—an aroma redolent with life.

But those on the way to destruction treat us more like the stench from a rotting corpse.

—2 Corinthians 2:15-16, MSG

When people are in the presence of Christ, who lives in us, those who are alive in Christ will smell life. But those who are dead in sin will smell death—their own! To suppress the truth of their own eternal death, they will do whatever it takes to silence those who proclaim Christ. Paul's own life was a testimony to this reality.

Five times I received at the hands of the Jews the forty lashes less one. Three times I was beaten with rods. Once I was stoned. Three times I was shipwrecked; a night and a day I was adrift at sea; on frequent journeys, in danger from rivers, danger from robbers, danger from my own people, danger from Gentiles, danger in the city, danger in the wilderness, danger at sea, danger from false brothers; in toil and hardship, through many a sleepless night, in hunger and thirst, often without food, cold and exposure. And, apart from other things, there is the daily pressure on me of my anxiety for all the churches.

—2 Corinthians 11:24-28

Because of his bold, unwavering witness, Paul suffered greatly for the gospel. But when we read the accounts of his missionary journeys in Acts or in his epistles, we don't get the sense he is purposely seeking out these sufferings for their own sake. When Paul was tormented by what he described as a "thorn in the flesh" and "messenger of Satan," he pleaded with God to remove it (2 Corinthians 12:7-9).

We can't know categorically whether this "thorn" was a demon, an enemy of his ministry, or a physical ailment. What is significant here is that Paul didn't seek after this thorn but was suffering from it as a result of living for Christ and that he pleaded repeatedly for God to take it away. Only when God for his own reasons and glory refused to take this suffering from him did Paul finally say:

> Therefore I will boast all the more gladly of my weaknesses, so that the power of Christ may rest upon me. For the sake of Christ, then, I am content with weaknesses, insults, hardships, persecutions, and calamities. For when I am weak, then I am strong.
>
> —2 Corinthians 12:9b-10

Out of a desire to be zealous for Christ, many believers, myself included, have felt a need to do radical things to provoke suffering or persecution. We hold some vague notion that this will prove to God how much we are devoted to him. Perhaps this idea is still hanging around subconsciously from the monastic era when sinners turned saints subjected themselves to extreme isolation, self-flagellation, starvation diets, and/or camel hair vests to prove their sanctification.

While I appreciate that many monks who practiced these things were godly men with good intentions, I wonder if they fully understood the theology of suffering. What I think they missed is that Jesus didn't call us to a lifestyle of self-inflicted isolation and suffering. Instead, he told us to go into the world to make disciples for him (Matthew 28:19-20). As we do that, suffering will inevitably find us.

TYPES OF SUFFERING WE MUST ACCEPT WITH MINISTRY

When we read through Paul's many sufferings in 2 Corinthians 11, we notice that suffering comes to Christ's disciples in different ways. Paul listed the physical hardships and dangers he willingly endured to take the gospel to those who had yet to hear. Traveling in Paul's time was a risky undertaking. On his missionary journeys, he faced violent storms, wild animals, and ruthless bandits. He often endured these trials with little food or shelter.

Cross-cultural missionaries today may travel to their ministry locations in comparative ease. But once on location, things can get challenging. This was certainly the case during my first missionary experience abroad. While the remote island in the Indian Ocean was definitely a beautiful place, there were also many physical hardships like extreme heat, mystery illnesses, malaria, theft, possible volcano eruptions, routine cuts of utility services, rodent infestations, and so on.

A high percentage of today's missionaries minister in far more urban settings, including huge, sprawling mega-cities. But these have their own set of physical trials and challenges from poor air quality, noise pollution, lack of green space, bumper-to-bumper traffic, unsafe public transportation, high poverty and crime rates, political unrest, etc. Taken individually, such challenges may not seem like much, but when dealing with them collectively day in and day out, they can wear on the body and soul.

Beyond that, most remaining unreached people groups are located in places that are politically and culturally challenging, difficult to travel to, and sometimes downright dangerous to live in. This is not a coincidence. There is a great need in the church today for men and women who like Paul are willing to embrace physical suffering so they can bring the gospel of Christ to these people.

Another kind of suffering is persecution. While we often think of persecution in physical terms, it doesn't usually start there. Often, persecution begins with words. People will try to stop our witness through persuasion, mockery, lies, and intimidation. The idea is to put us in our place and use social pressure to cow us into compliance.

If this fails, they will often ramp up the social pressure by distancing us from the community. This can look like anything from being shunned by a peer group to being disowned by one's family. This stage of persecution could mean a loss of employment, being put in jail, or losing one's children, depending on where one lives.

If this approach still doesn't achieve the desired results, people may resort to actual physical violence, assuming as Satan did with Job that we value our bodies more than our souls. Whether physical beatings, mob attacks, destruction of property, imprisonment, or actual killing of believers by extremist government regimes and religious groups, these are the last desperate attempts to stop the spread of the gospel.

In fact, it was because Paul steadfastly refused to stop preaching the gospel of Christ that he found himself in a dungeon, waiting to be executed. But we can take courage in our persecution, knowing that while our bodies may be locked up or killed, there is absolutely no way to stop the advancement of the kingdom of God, as Paul assured Timothy.

Remember Jesus Christ, risen from the dead, the offspring of David, as preached in my gospel, for which I am suffering, bound with chains as a criminal. But the word of God is not bound!

—2 Timothy 2:8-9

There is another way we can suffer for the gospel, and that is by investing our hearts and lives into others as we make disciples for Christ. Paul exhorts Timothy to do just that.

And what you have heard from me in the presence of many witnesses entrust to faithful men who will be able to teach others also.

—2 Timothy 2:2

This is what discipleship is all about. It is like a stream falling down the descending steps of a waterfall. As people pour the gospel and their lives into us, we in turn pour the gospel and ourselves out into others. As we do this, we begin to care for these new believers and disciples, pray for them, and feel a parental responsibility for their spiritual development.

There is a joy in watching children grow. But there is also a weight parents feel as they try to ensure that their children become adults who are physically, emotionally, and spiritually healthy. This was the pressure Paul described beyond the physical hardships he endured when he added, "And apart from other things, there is the daily pressure on me of my anxiety for all the churches" (2 Corinthians 11:28)

Anyone who has ever invested themselves into others as they've pastored a community, led a small group, or mentored a young believer understands the kind of concern and anxiety Paul expressed for the churches he planted. Investing in others is often a heavy burden. But it is also an incredible privilege to suffer in this way.

REFLECT AND APPLY

How much are you willing to suffer for the gospel? Is this an area that needs some maturing in your life?

CHAPTER NINETEEN
SUFFERING HARDSHIPS WITH PURPOSE

Suffer hardship with me, as a good soldier of Christ Jesus. No soldier in active service entangles himself in the affairs of everyday life, so that he may please the one who enlisted him as a soldier. Also if anyone competes as an athlete, he does not win the prize unless he competes according to the rules. The hard-working farmer ought to be the first to receive his share of the crops.

—2 Timothy 2:3-4

A LIFE OF SERVICE TO GOD WILL MEAN A LIFE of sacrifice for God. We need to come to grips with this and embrace it because only through enduring hardships will we reach the end goal of gospel transformation in the lives into whom we pour ourselves. If we keep this focus clear in our minds, we can bear hardships gladly, as uncomfortable as they may be, knowing it is more than worth it.

This idea of purposefully sacrificing in our present circumstances for a greater payoff in the future is something people do all the time. So why wouldn't we also do this for the sake of the gospel? A good soldier chooses to make personal sacrifices for the advancement of his country and to please his commanding officer. A competitive athlete chooses to suffer the pain of physical training because he longs for the championship title. A hard-working farmer chooses to endure the heat of the sun for the dream of harvesting a bumper crop. Each of these people subjects themselves to hardship, but they do so purposefully and even willingly for the gain they hope to receive.

THE GOOD SOLDIER

My father and several of my friends have served in various branches of the military. I've heard enough of their experiences to know that watching a war movie like *Hacksaw Ridge* doesn't qualify me to write about the suffering of soldiers. They make sacrifices on and off the battlefield I will never fully grasp. So I asked a friend of mine who has done three tours of duty to share with me his perspective on this topic.

Surprisingly, he didn't speak much about the hardships of serving in a war zone but on how his family suffered because of his decision to re-enlist. At the time, he was between a completed deployment to Iraq and an upcoming deployment to Afghanistan. Unlike prior deployments, the choice to re-enlist was his to make as his military contract would run out before his date of deployment. He wrote the following about the internal struggle he faced.

> I had completed a deployment to Iraq and in some measure felt like I had fulfilled my contract with the military. I had chosen to join the military when I was eighteen and single. Now I was married with one child and a second on the way. Would I automatically be a bad father and husband if I chose to go? About a month later, I signed my contract and chose a path that would cause our family to suffer.[1]

There were various reasons why he chose to re-enlist. But one that stood out was his conviction that while serving in America's military was a choice, it was also an obligation to his country.

THE COMPETITIVE ATHLETE

In high school, I had the privilege of playing for a very competitive soccer team. Tryouts for this team started mid-August, but the pain and suffering started much earlier. At the beginning of summer, the coach would mail us a training schedule we had to follow if we didn't want to embarrass ourselves at tryouts. I was free to do anything I wanted with my summers, but I willingly chose to follow his training plan.

While this involved subjecting myself to a lot of physical suffering, I didn't think of it as a burden to bear. I was happy to run sprints, practice foot drills, and give up any other activity that would get in the way of playing for my team. I remember my experience on that team as one of the best times of my life. Though I recall the brutal practices, I can't help but smile because I also remember what it felt like to bring home championship trophies.

THE HARDWORKING FARMER

Being a farmer is not a nine-to-five job but a way of life. I realized this during my time ministering amongst an agriculturalist people group in Tanzania, East Africa. Even after the men stepped away from their fields, all they wanted to talk about was how the weather was affecting their crops or what new seed the government was promoting that year. If I was ever going to connect with these people, I realized I needed to enter into their world of farming. So I bought a good hoe and worked alongside them in their fields, bent over in the blazing heat.

As I worked with them and saw the challenges they faced, I knew I wanted to be part of collectively solving these problems. Since I was clueless on how to go about doing that, I traveled to a demonstration farm in South Africa to glean what I could. My time there was very profitable, and I learned enough about sustainable agriculture to know that developing the sandy dirt found in our village into healthy soil was going to take a lot of work.

But now I knew how to do it, at least in theory, and I wanted to show the villagers and myself what could happen if we worked hard and implemented sustainable farming methods. To do this, I decided to make a demonstration plot in my front yard since it bordered the main road going through the village. This involved planting a living wall of Moringa trees around my maize plot and meticulously following the sustainable techniques I'd learned in South Africa. I can assure you this was a lot harder than anything I'd experienced working in the local fields. But I subjected myself to blistered hands and aching muscles because I believed I would get a harvest that people would have to take notice of.

And I did. Not because of any brilliance on my part but because I worked hard and followed the directions of my South African agricultural instructors. At the end of the growing season, many people stopped by to tell me I had the best-looking corn in the entire village. And when I looked out over my plot from the shade of my porch, I could honestly say those tall, luscious stalks of maize were well worth the blistered hands and sore muscles it took to produce them.

PAIN WITHOUT PURPOSE IS PAIN WITH NO GAIN

In all of the examples Paul gives us, we see that anything in life that is worthwhile is also going to demand a certain amount of sacrifice and suffering. Purposeful suffering is a strategic choice, not an end to itself. What would be the point of following my coach's grueling training schedule all summer if I never expected to try out for the soccer team? It would make no sense to endure all that pain without any expectation of gain.

Paul applies this same logic to God's kingdom. If we want to see the gain of a spiritual harvest in our ministry, we must first suffer the pain of enduring hardships. Choosing to live a life of sacrifice for God is certainly not an easy endeavor, but we suffer purposefully, knowing that "in due season we will reap, if we do not give up" (Galatians 6:9).

REFLECT AND APPLY

Do you tend to endure hardships in your life because you are intentionally choosing a life of sacrifice or for other reasons? Going forward, how will you purposefully make sacrifices with the end goal of reaping a spiritual harvest?

CHAPTER TWENTY
OUR RESPONSE TO SUFFERING AND SHAME

For God gave us a spirit not of fear but of power and love and self-control. Therefore do not be ashamed of the testimony about our Lord, nor of me his prisoner, but share in suffering for the gospel by the power of God.

—2 Timothy 1:7-8

PAUL KNEW THAT THE DESIRE TO AVOID SHAME had the potential to keep Timothy from taking up his share of suffering for the gospel. Shame and its partner fear are both very human responses to the potential of suffering for Christ. In intense moments of conflict over our faith, the natural reaction is to run away from physical danger and/or hide from social condemnation.

In both cases, what we are ultimately doing is trying to protect ourselves from death, either the death of our bodies or the death of our reputation. No matter what culture people come from, their bodies and their honor are very high on the list of things they cherish and protect. Our adversaries will try to leverage this desire for self-preservation to manipulate us into distancing ourselves from Christ.

Knowing this, how do we ensure that we don't default to shame and fear in these moments of suffering? In the above verses, Paul gives us the answer. First, we align ourselves with Christ and his people. Second, we rely on the power of God.

ALIGN WITH CHRIST AND HIS PEOPLE

When Paul tells Timothy not to be ashamed of the testimony of God or of Paul himself as a prisoner (2 Timothy 1:8), he does so in the context of seeing many in his faith community get as far away from him as they can. They are doing this in part because they are afraid, but Paul also mentions repeatedly the concept of acting out of shame (2 Timothy 1:15-16). The

Greek word Paul uses for shame is *epaischunomai,* which conveys the idea of "being disgraced because of wrongly identifying with something."

Groups of people that associate together typically have commonly held values, whether they can communicate them or not. When a member of a community does something contrary to these collective values, the group will usually make their disapproval known to the offender. The threat of this is often enough to keep most people adhering to the group values, at least outwardly.

A good example of this is the Amish and Old Order Mennonite communities that came from the Anabaptist movement and settled in Pennsylvania in the seventeenth century. From observing their lifestyle during my college years in Lancaster, Pennsylvania, I've come to recognize that they understand more than most what it means to align one's identity to their faith community instead of the world.

That said, perhaps it is because they are constantly thinking through how much of the world's culture should be adopted into their own faith culture that they have historically been prone to factions and sub-groups. In many Amish and Old Order Mennonite communities, any time a group holds a different set of values than the majority, they are shamed into conformity. If this fails, they will often be forced to leave the community.

The denomination in which I grew up came to exist when a group of young adults were pressured to leave the Mennonite Brethren in Christ. The official story according to church documents is that this break was due to reasons of "ecclesiology and personality differences." But according to church lore, it happened because of a prayer meeting. Specifically, this group of young adults began meeting to pray on Wednesday nights, which was not sanctioned by the elders.

To make matters worse, they were also raising their hands during prayer, something considered shameful by the older generations at this time. Never mind the fact that Paul cautioned the Roman church against arguing over which day to worship God and actually advocated lifting hands during prayer, as was common in Jewish and early church culture.

> One person esteems one day as better than another, while another esteems all days alike. Each one should be fully convinced in his own mind.
>
> —Romans 14:5

> I desire then that in every place the men should pray, lifting holy hands without anger or quarreling.
>
> —1 Timothy 1:8

What it really came down to was the fact that these practices were not part of the elder church members' faith culture at that time. Because these young adults were not willing to back down from their convictions to meet when they felt "fully convinced" to meet or to "lift holy hands" in prayer, they were eventually pressured to leave the community.

This account from my own faith heritage shows the power communities can have over our lives through shame when we don't comply with their standards. These youth aligned themselves with each other, which allowed them to endure the shaming by their elders. For them, conformity to the legalism of the elders would have been the real shame because it would mean turning away from the values held by their own genuine community. That was why Paul called out Phygelus and Hermogenes when they pulled away from him.

> You are aware that all who are in Asia turned away from me, among whom are Phygelus and Hermogenes. May the Lord grant mercy to the household of Onesiphorus, for he often refreshed me and was not ashamed of my chains.
>
> —2 Timothy 1:15-16

These two men were claiming to align themselves with Christ. But their actions of distancing themselves from Paul showed that they were actually ashamed of him. By feeling the shame imposed by Nero and Rome, they were showing very clearly with whom they were actually aligning themselves.

Onesiphorus, on the other hand, was not ashamed of Paul even though Paul was a prisoner of Nero and Rome. The way Onesiphorus sought out Paul and ministered to him showed who he considered to be his true community. In his letter, Paul reminded Timothy that his place was with Christ and other believers. As such, the only shame he should be feeling was if by his action he was not aligning himself with his faith community.

WE RELY ON THE POWER OF GOD

It is vital to realize now that we will be unable to stand on our own strength in moments of suffering and persecution. We will either cave to the pressures put upon us or we will try to muster up our own courage and resolve. Either way, we will fall short because neither one brings honor to Christ, which is the goal of suffering. Our aim is not to just "hold it together" or "not be an embarrassment" but to bring glory to God by allowing the moment to be his and not ours. We can only do this when his Spirit of Power manifests himself in us. This is why Paul urges Timothy to "share in suffering for the gospel **by the power of God**" (2 Timothy 1:8). Paul reiterates this vital truth to the Corinthian church.

> For he [Christ] was crucified in weakness, but lives by the power of God. For we also are weak in him, but in dealing with you we will live with him by the power of God.
>
> —2 Corinthians 13:4

We are reminded in this verse of our weakness but also that in our weakness we can live for Christ through God's power, i.e., the Holy Spirit. This is true in everyday situations but especially true in moments when we are suffering for Christ. Jesus told his disciples:

> And you will be dragged before governors and kings for my sake, to bear witness before them and the Gentiles. When they deliver you over, do not be anxious how you are to speak or what you are to say, for what you are to say will be given to you in that hour. For it is not you who speak, but the Spirit of your Father speaking through you.
>
> —Matthew 10:18-20

If we are followers of Christ, then that promise is for us too. We can't know what kind of suffering we may have to endure for Christ, nor should we be unduly preoccupied with the possibilities. We should instead prepare ourselves ahead of time to face any kind of suffering by nurturing a lifestyle of dependence on God's Spirit, who gives us the power we need in these moments. Paul understood this principle when he wrote to the church of Corinth:

> I didn't come to you with brilliant speeches or persuasive words but in weakness and with a powerful demonstration of the Holy Spirit.
>
> —1 Corinthians 2:1, HCSB

In other words, it won't be our well-crafted arguments, stiff upper lip, or courage that will draw others to Christ in the moments of our suffering but a demonstration of God's Spirit through us. I confess I put off writing this section of the book for a couple of weeks because I was afraid just writing about suffering might somehow heap extra portions of it on my life. But as I studied God's Word, I realized that while suffering is not something I naturally gravitate towards, it's something I need to see as a normal part of life if I am a disciple of Christ.

If there has been a long period in your life without any suffering for Christ, his gospel, or his servants, it would be prudent to ask the Holy Spirit to empower you to step up and accept your share. As you do this, remember to resist the impulse to create forced situations of suffering. If you are living and proclaiming the gospel, it will naturally come to you. Jesus promises it!

REFLECT AND APPLY

Do you feel shame when people give you pushback about your faith in Jesus? What does this tell you about who you are aligning with in this world?

GOING DEEPER

SUGGESTED ACTIVITIES

1. Learn more about the persecuted church throughout the world. A good place to start is at the Voice of the Martyrs website, www.persecution.com. Stand with them by praying and fasting for them. Consider how else you can partner with those who are working with the persecuted church.

2. Meditate on the Passion of Christ by visiting and praying through the Stations of the Cross (also known as the Way of the Cross). This series of pictures depicting the events surrounding Jesus's death can be found in churches, cemeteries, hospitals, and spiritual retreat centers.

3. Like the hardworking farmer, plant a small garden. Put in the work and time of tending the garden throughout the growing season with the expectation of eating food that you have grown. Reflect on the correlation of that experience and intentional sacrifice for God's kingdom work.

SUGGESTED READING:

      The Insanity of God by Nik Ripken

      Tried by Fire by William J. Bennett

SECTION SIX:

A VESSEL FOR GOD'S SERVICE

O merciful Father, do not consider what we have done against you;
But what our blessed Savior has done for us.
Don't consider what we have made of ourselves,
But what He is making of us for you, our God.
O that Christ may be "wisdom and righteousness, sanctification and
*   redemption*
To every one of our souls.
May His precious blood cleanse us from all our sins,
And your Holy Spirit renew and sanctify our souls.
May He crucify our flesh with its passion and lusts,
And cleanse all our brothers and sisters in Christ across the earth.
Amen."

—John Wesley,
Leader of a revival movement within the
Church of England known today as Methodism

CHAPTER TWENTY-ONE
BECOMING SET-APART VESSELS

Now in a great house there are not only vessels of gold and silver but also of wood and clay, some for honorable use, some for dishonorable. Therefore, if anyone cleanses himself from what is dishonorable, he will be a vessel for honorable use, set apart as holy, useful to the master of the house, ready for every good work.

—2 Timothy 2:20-21

WEALTHY, INFLUENTIAL PEOPLE OF PAUL'S DAY lived in large, single-family houses called *domus*, the same Latin word from which we get the English word *domestic*. These houses had courtyards, running water, and in-floor heating systems. Sprawling, high-ceilinged rooms were typically decorated with fresco paintings on the walls, mosaic tiles on the floors, and ornate furniture. Serving bowls, goblets, platters, and utensils might be made of silver or even gold.

But not everything was glitz and glamour. However wealthy, these elite engaged in normal human activities like eating and relieving themselves. So a *domus* also contained everyday items like cooking utensils, storage containers, and chamber pots. Because servants used these items for daily chores, they would typically be made of wood or clay and kept out of sight. These common containers existed in a very different world from highly-valued vessels of silver and gold displayed in main living areas and available for the master's personal use.[1]

HONORABLE VS. DISHONORABLE VESSEL

King Solomon once referenced "a word fitly spoken" as being like golden apples displayed in an ornate silver bowl (Proverbs 25:11). Such a magnificent vessel would be something displayed before this great king's special guests. We might imagine the Queen of Sheba commenting, "Look at those delicious apples sitting in that exquisite silver bowl."

According to Scripture, King Solomon made Israel so prosperous that during his reign silver became as common as stone in Jerusalem (1 Kings 10:27). Still, I'm sure Solomon would have felt a certain amount of pride over how this beautiful silver vessel complemented the gold of the apples. Such a bowl is useful to the master of the home because it both serves a practical purpose and brings him the honor he deserves.

In contrast to this "honorable" vessel is another "dishonorable" vessel that is kept tucked away from visitors: the chamber pot. If you aren't familiar with this device, think of a large bowl that can sit in the seat of a chair or be used independently as a toilet. The chamber pot was typically made of clay because this was a cheap material that also has the very important characteristic of being waterproof. [2] A chamber pot would be filthy and pungent after being used all day by the master's family.

Now let's reimagine our Queen of Sheba story. The queen arrives at Solomon's palace after a long, dusty caravan journey. After freshening up, she goes to greet the wise, larger-than-life King Solomon. After formal introductions and exchange of gifts, the two monarchs settle in for a lengthy conversation. Right on cue, the king's servants bring out those beautiful golden apples. But instead of a silver bowl, this time they are presented in a crusty, fly-covered chamber pot.

You can imagine the disgust on the queen's face and the shame King Solomon would feel. The servant responsible for this mishap would pay severely. Why? Even to the lowliest of servants, it should be self-evident that you don't use disgusting, dishonorable vessels for distinguished, honorable purposes. Ever!

Becoming Repurposed for God's Use

Why would God want to use someone who is filling their life with this world's excrement? If God is choosing a vessel to use for his kingdom purposes, and on the shelf he sees one clean, shiny vessel and a second dirty, dull one, for which vessel do you think he will reach? For which one would you reach? The answer should be obvious. If you want God to use you, then you need to prepare yourself by living a life that is pure, honorable, and ready for our Master's reach.

It's easy to agree with that last statement. But when we examine the sin in our lives, we can admit we often feel more like a toilet bowl than a fruit bowl. We are soiled vessels, and we may fear we are now doomed to live a life of dishonor hidden away in some back cupboard of our Master's house. That is what Satan would like us to believe. But as seen in the above passage, it doesn't have to be the case. We can cleanse ourselves and become honorable once again in God's sight. The apostle John tells us how in his first epistle.

> If we confess our sins, he is faithful and just to forgive us our sins and to cleanse us from all unrighteousness.
>
> —1 John 1:9

In other words, a dirty, broken vessel can be cleaned up and repurposed for something useful and honorable. According to one documentary on chamber pots, antique collectors have been doing this unknowingly for years.[3] Mistakenly thinking ornate chamber pots once owned by wealthy aristocrats and royalty were gravy boats or punch bowls, they've purchased them from antique shops and cleaned them up to use on special occasions. This may sound revolting at first. But there could hardly be a better example of how God rescued and redeemed us for his purposes. The power of the gospel can turn chamber pots full of sinful refuse into beautiful bowls full of the fruit of the Holy Spirit.

REFLECT AND APPLY

What excrement of this world are you filling your life with that is preventing the Holy Spirit from purifying you and God to use you in new ways for his kingdom?

CHAPTER TWENTY-TWO
BECOMING A PURE VESSEL

Now in a large house, there are not only gold and silver bowls but also those of wood and clay, some for honorable use, some for dishonorable. So if anyone purifies himself from anything dishonorable, he will be a special instrument, set apart, useful to the Master, prepared for every good work.— 2 Timothy 2:20-21 (HCSB)

Flee from youthful passions, and pursue righteousness, faith, love, and peace, along with those who call on the Lord from a pure heart.

—2 Timothy 2:22

AS PAUL ADMONISHED TIMOTHY ABOVE, if we want to be pure vessels ready to be used by the Master, we need to be intentional about fleeing "youthful passions." This phrase doesn't just encompass sexual temptations but all the worldly desires people spend their youthful energies chasing. The apostle John categorized these passions into three groups.

> For everything in the world—the lust of the flesh, the lust of the eyes, and the pride of life—comes not from the Father but from the world.
>
> —1 John 2:16, NIV

Because these passions can so quickly sideline us in life and in ministry, it's important to examine what they are and why they are so dangerous. After all, it's only possible to flee from something if we're aware of its presence and recognize it as a serious threat.

LUST OF THE FLESH

Lust of the flesh can be defined as enjoying the good things of God outside their proper context or in excess. As Christ's servants, we usually feel a healthy pressure from God and those we serve to practice what we preach by abstaining from obvious lusts of the flesh such as illegal drugs, prostitution, pornography, and drunken revelry. But what about just having a couple more "adult" beverages than we should at a gathering? Or reaching for one more donut at the board meeting? Or escaping into social media when we should be engaging with our family?

Because these things aren't necessarily wrong in and of themselves and other people typically ignore "minor" infractions, it isn't always obvious when we've crossed the line into excess. But as this happens, we begin to undermine the gospel we preach and God's ability to use us as vessels for his service. That's why it's so important to intentionally seek out others whom the Holy Spirit can use to call us out when they see us living in unbalanced ways. Not having regular outside accountability invites the lusts of the flesh into our lives and ministry.

LUST OF THE EYES

Lust of the eyes is when we obsess over things others have because we want them. This might include coveting someone else's spiritual gifts, attractive spouse, house size, or popularity. The list could go on endlessly. What isn't a big deal to one person can bring on a serious case of envy in another. The core issue isn't what we are lusting after but falsely seeing that thing as something we need instead of learning to be content with what God has given us. As believers, our attitude should be like the apostle Paul's.

> Not that I am speaking of being in need, for I have learned in whatever situation I am to be content. I know how to be brought low, and I know how to abound. In any and every circumstance, I have learned the secret of facing plenty and hunger, abundance and need. I can do all things through him who strengthens me.
>
> —Philippians 4:11-13

Paul learned to live in the illusive state of contentment because he understood that everyone is needy in some areas while well off in others and that both situations have blessings as well as challenges. Paul understood that the key to contentment in all circumstances is learning to live interdependently with others instead of in competition. As God changes our perspective, we come to see both need and abundance as opportunities to bless and be blessed. In the areas where we are well off, we stop hoarding because we now see our abundance as an opportunity to bless others. As we give out of our extra, we realize there is a joy and freedom that comes from being a dispenser of God's resources.

But what about when we find ourselves on the other side of the equation? In those times of need, we humble ourselves and allow others the blessing of helping us out of their abundance as Paul himself does immediately after expressing his contentment.

> Yet it was kind of you to share my trouble . . . I am well supplied, having received from Epaphroditus the gifts you sent, a fragrant offering, a sacrifice acceptable and pleasing to God.
>
> —Philippians 4:14, 18b

So whether in need or abundance, we bless and are blessed in Christ. When we live this out practically like the early church in Jerusalem who "were of one heart and soul" and considered all their resources to be communal property (Acts 4:32-34), then we stop coveting one another's extras. Instead, we understand the blessing of using our abundance to live sustainably together. At that moment, the lust of the eyes is replaced with gratefulness and contentment in our hearts.

THE PRIDE OF LIFE

The last group of fleshly passions the apostle John mentions is the pride of life. This is when we seek personal identity and glory through achievement, position, or fame. The pride of life is a very difficult giant to slay, but in God's strength this giant must fall. God has no use for ministers who are seeking to bolster their own identity through their ministries. He especially has no time for those who become full of pride and self-reliance. We either willingly humble ourselves before God, or he will do it for us. Be forewarned that God's way usually involves an intense spiral downward before God then brings you back up.

If we could excuse anyone for being full of himself, it might be Joseph, the beloved son of Jacob, patriarchal father of the Israelites (Genesis 37-50). Most things people spend their youth chasing came to him naturally. A wealthy family. Good looks. Designer clothes. His father's favoritism. Even a highly-sought-after life skill—the gift of telling the future through dreams.

Joseph had done little to deserve or earn these things, and that was part of his problem. Since he'd never had to go through the normal struggles of life, he lacked the humility and responsibility to steward what God had given him. Instead, he was just a spoiled, prideful young man. Gifted? Extremely. But not an honorable vessel that God could use.

At least that was the case before God got ahold of Joseph and slowly but surely broke him of his pride. This process was literally the pits (pun intended). It started with his jealous older brothers tossing him into a Canaanite pit and ended with him being locked up in an Egyptian pit. The first pit would lead to eleven years of slavery while the second one saw him serving two years for an attempted rape charge of which he was innocent.

On the surface, this period of Joseph's life seems unfair and a waste. But God used the evil actions of others to strip Joseph of his pride and purify him to become a vessel fit for God's purpose. Only then would God use Joseph to save his people and that entire region from a seven-year famine.

In the end, Joseph could see that it was God who arranged these events in order to use him in a very honorable way. Joseph's story isn't a rags-to-riches tale like Aladdin but a true account of how God takes care of his people in miraculous ways. It also makes clear that God is not interested in using people, no matter how gifted, until they have put to death the pride of life.

REFLECT AND APPLY

Why is the pride of life the last youthful passion that tends to be dealt with in our quest to be pure vessels?

CHAPTER TWENTY-THREE
BECOMING A PREPARED VESSEL

Now in a large house, there are not only gold and silver bowls but also those of wood and clay, some for honorable use, some for dishonorable. So if anyone purifies himself from anything dishonorable, he will be a special instrument, set apart, useful to the Master, prepared for every good work.

—*2 Timothy 2:20-21 (HCSB)*

Therefore, my beloved, as you have always obeyed, so now, not only as in my presence but much more in my absence, work out your own salvation with fear and trembling, for it is God who works in you, both to will and to work for his good pleasure.

—*Philippians 2:12-13*

LET ME SHARE A CONFESSION OF MY OWN. Regrettably, I spent my teen years chasing after the lust of the flesh and most of my adult life chasing after the lust of the eyes and pride of life. I wish I could blame this on ignorance, but in truth I knew better. As a young boy, I loved God and even responded to his call in my early teens to give my life to cross-cultural missions.

But throughout high school until my junior year of college, I decided I wanted to live life on my own terms. I figured I could get serious about my faith and calling to missions after I graduated from college. This flawed attitude was only made worse by relative success playing high school and college soccer. As my foot skills improved, so did my standing with the ladies. I eventually found myself with two overarching youthful passions: sports and the opposite gender. I chased both with abandon, and soon they defined my life.

This all came to an end my junior year of college when my heavenly Father's patience ran out. In his grace, he helped me to remove the gods I'd set up in my life by giving me a broken heart and a busted-up leg. A relationship I'd thought would end in marriage fell apart. And a serious knee injury ended any hopes of playing soccer or even walking for three months.

During that time of immobility, I did little else but study and pray. Through this experience, I fell in love with God again. For a number of years, I experienced his unending joy in my life. It felt almost as though I'd been born again, again!

At some point though, God deeply convicted me that much of my internal life still resembled a chamber pot. That conviction wasn't a bad thing, but my solution to it was. I tried to use the character traits that had helped me excel up to that point, will power and determination, to clean up my internal life. What started off as a healthy desire for purity quickly developed into a lifestyle of behavior modification through rules and personal effort.

The result was a life that looked good from the outside but was often full of legalism and lacked any real power from God's Spirit. Looking back, I wonder how much of my good works from that time, fueled mostly by my own energies, will someday burn up like wood, hay, and stubble as the apostle Paul warned (1 Corinthians 3:12-13). It is a mistake common to many Christians. As Christian author and pastor John Piper puts it:

> The great problem in contemporary Christian living is not learning the right things to do but how to do the right things.[1]
>
> —John Piper

That was my problem. I knew I was supposed to "flee youthful passions," but I hadn't gone on to "pursue righteousness, faith, love, and peace, along with those who call on the Lord from a pure heart" (2 Timothy 2:22). This was something I wouldn't figure out until years later when I received a fresh filling of God's Spirit. At that point, God, not me, put within me a pure heart that desired to produce his fruit.

Learning to Follow the Spirit's Lead

In his epistle to the Galatians, the apostle Paul gives us a description of what it means to live as a pure vessel filled by the Holy Spirit and producing Holy Spirit fruit.

> But if you are led by the Spirit, you are not under the law . . . But the fruit of the Spirit is love, joy, peace, patience, kindness, goodness, faithfulness, gentleness, self-control; against such things there is no law. And those who belong to Christ Jesus have crucified the flesh with its passions and desires. If we live by the Spirit, let us also walk by the Spirit.
>
> —Galatians 5:18, 22-25

Paul's whole point in this passage is that we can't law ourselves into God's kingdom, into God's good graces, or into being people filled with the fruit of the Spirit. That can only happen as we are led by the Holy Spirit. We discussed earlier how we receive God's Spirit when we come to Christ, but that's not the same as living full of the Spirit (see chapter ten). We often want to enjoy the fresh life the Holy Spirit gives without also submitting to the Spirit's total headship. Some believers revert back to living in the flesh. Others after tasting the freedom of Christ return to living under the law.

That is why Paul reminds us to both "live by the Spirit" and "walk by the Spirit" (Galatians 5:25). In the original Greek, the phrase *walk by* can also be translated *follow*. This same Greek verb can be used to describe three different but similar situations: a conductor leading an orchestra, a shepherd leading his flock, and a sergeant leading his men in a march.

Hopefully, you can connect with at least one of these analogies. But all three highlight the same truth. Our walking with the Spirit only works when we learn to take our cues from him and totally submit to his leadership.

So what does it mean to walk with the Spirit on a practical level? Where does his role of leading end and my responsibility to follow start? If the Holy Spirit is putting his desires in me, is my role totally passive, or is there something that God is expecting me to do? Our second focus passage for this chapter gives insight into these questions.

> Therefore, my beloved, as you have always obeyed, so now, not only as in my presence but much more in my absence, work out your own salvation with fear and trembling, for it is God who works in you, both to will and to work for his good pleasure.
>
> —Philippians 2:12-13

This passage tells us that God gives us the desire and power to do his will, but he also expects us to be a part of that process. He wants us to "work out" our salvation by submitting to his will and guidance. This is an obedience that flows from God's grace and not man's law.

Spiritual Disciplines as a Means of Grace

Spiritual disciplines are intentional practices you can incorporate into your life in order to "work out your own salvation" (v. 12). If implemented under the guidance of the Holy Spirit and with the right heart attitude, these disciplines can help you grow spiritually. They can be divided into three groups: inward, outward, and corporate. Inward disciplines include meditation, prayer, fasting, and study. Outward include simplicity, solitude, and submission. Corporate disciplines are done in community and include confession, worship, guidance, and celebration.

Jesus's original Jewish audience was familiar with these spiritual disciplines, so Jesus didn't need to explain what they were but only how to redeem them. A good example is fasting. Fasting was a common religious practice in Jesus's day, so when he spoke of fasting, he didn't need to dwell on its technical aspects. Instead, he focused on heart attitudes such as why we fast (Matthew 6:16-18). Do we fast so others will notice us and think we are religious people? Or is it done in a way that honors God and seeks a treasure from him alone?

For twenty-first century readers of the Bible, a potential dilemma is understanding what many of these disciplines looked like in their original contexts. Thankfully, we can find a wealth of practical knowledge in our collective church history. *Sacred Rhythms* by Ruth Haley Barton is one contemporary title that has gathered the wisdom of the past for our use today. I would highly recommend having it on your shelf and returning to it periodically.

Another potential dilemma as you explore spiritual disciplines may be the temptation to implement all of them at once or not do any until they can be done perfectly. The remedy for both is to start your spiritual discipline journey by implementing a few at a time with consistency and purpose. In this manner, you will not only ensure actually starting your journey but will be encouraged with your progress as you allow the Holy Spirit to lead you deeper.

One last caution is to keep in mind that these disciplines are just tools. It is the Holy Spirit who does the inward transformation. The usefulness of spiritual disciplines is in their ability to get us into God's presence and in a state where we can connect with him in ever-deepening ways. That is why John Wesley called them "means of grace." Practicing them contributes to receiving the Holy Spirit's filling and fruit. The equations below have helped bring clarity to the truths of 2 Timothy 2:20-22.

Holy Spirit Desire + Spiritual Disciplines = Fruit Bowl

a pure vessel on the outside and full of the fruit of the Spirit inside

Legalism + Spiritual Disciplines = Toilet Bowl

a pure vessel in appearance on the outside but full of legalism and self inside

REFLECT AND APPLY

We are called to live by the Spirit and walk by the Spirit. In what areas of your life are you not fully submitting to the Holy Spirit's headship?

GOING DEEPER

SUGGESTED ACTIVITIES

1. Choose a spiritual discipline to learn more about, then choose one small way you can immediately and whole-heartedly implement it into your life.

2. Just as Christ wants to repurpose us into new vessels, find something that needs repurposing and work at turning it into something functional and beautiful. At the completion of the project, reflect on how this process is similar to your own transformation.

3. Paul suffered a burden for the churches as he prayed for them (2 Corinthians 11:28). Begin praying for your church daily or weekly and see if the Holy Spirit doesn't begin to put a stronger burden for your church on your heart.

SUGGESTED READING:

Sacred Rhythms by Ruth Haley Barton

Spiritual Disciplines for the Christian Life by Donald S. Whitney

SECTION SEVEN:
THE WORD OF TRUTH

Your words are perfect, O Lord. They are refreshing to my soul. Your testimony is trustworthy. It is perfect and gives wisdom to the simple. Your doctrines are right. They make my heart full of joy because they are pure. Your commands are radiant, they give light to my eyes. To fear you Lord is good and cleansing to my soul. Your rules are solid and always righteous. They are more to be desired than gold, even much fine gold. They are also sweeter than honey and drippings of the honeycomb. Moreover, by them I am warned and greatly rewarded. Who can discern his errors? Declare me innocent from hidden faults and keep me from presumptuous sins; let them not rule over me! Then I will be blameless, and innocent of great sin. Let the words of my mouth and the meditation of my heart be acceptable in your sight, O Lord, my rock and my redeemer.

—King David, a prayer paraphrased from Psalm 19

CHAPTER TWENTY-FOUR
EQUIPPING US FOR MINISTRY

Evil people and imposters will become worse, deceiving and being deceived. But as for you, continue in what you have learned and have firmly believed, knowing from whom you learned it and how from childhood you have been acquainted with the sacred writings, which are able to make you wise for salvation through faith in Christ Jesus. All scripture is inspired by God, and profitable for teaching, for rebuking, for correcting, for training in righteousness, so that the man of God may be complete, equipped for every good work.

—2 Timothy 3:13-16

THE ENGLISH WORD *HERESY* ORIGINATES FROM THE Greek word *hairesis,* which means "a choice"— as in "a choice that all professing believers have to either hold fast to the truths found in God's Word or walk away from them into error." This is a choice both individuals and churches of every generation need to make. Will we allow the world's philosophies to creep into our doctrine? Will we permit man-made rules and traditions to be added on to the gospel? It's easy to drift into these and other false teachings if we aren't alert enough to recognize them or zealous enough to battle them when they try to creep into our congregations.

THE CHURCH'S TENDENCY TOWARDS HERESY

Around 57 A.D., the apostle Paul was headed to Jerusalem from Macedonia when he made a stop on the windy shores of what is modern-day Turkey. His purpose was to gather the Ephesian elders and explain his Holy Spirit-led compulsion to go to Jerusalem as well as to deliver a prophetic warning to the church of Ephesus concerning heresies (Acts 20:17-38). He warned them that "savage wolves" (v. 29) would come into their community to spread false teachings. He encouraged them to stay alert as men from their own congregation would try to lure members away with deviant doctrines (v. 30). He also told the elders they'd never see his face again on this side of heaven because "imprisonment and afflictions" (v. 23) awaited him in Jerusalem.

Though Paul spent most of his farewell speech talking about the dangers of heresies, it seems all the elders could focus on was that they'd never see him again, weeping bitterly as they made their farewells. Perhaps in consequence, it only took about six years according to biblical scholars for Paul's prophetic words to come true. In fact, the apostle John's first letter to the churches in Revelation, believed to have been written almost forty years after Paul's stop here, calls out the church of Ephesus for having abandoned their first love and pleads with them to repent (Revelation 2:1-7).

We know the passage of time from Paul's meeting with the Ephesian elders was no more than six years since his travel to Jerusalem, arrest, captivity under Roman governor Felix, appeal to Caesar, and transport to Rome covered an estimated four years, followed by two more years of house arrest (Acts 20-28). At the end of these two years, it appears Paul was released at least temporarily since his first letter to Timothy references a trip to Macedonia. By this point, many people in the Ephesian church had already lost their focus on the gospel and were listening to false teachers and quarreling over speculative myths and genealogies (1 Timothy 1:3-5; 2 Timothy 4:4). These heresies were why Paul urged Timothy:

> Remain at Ephesus so that you may charge certain persons not to teach any different doctrine, nor to devote themselves to myths and endless genealogies, which promote speculations.
>
> —1 Timothy 1:3-4

Paul's charge to Timothy was for him to take a church that was dabbling in heresy and turn them into truth seekers. This was no simple task as seen in the significant amount of ink Paul used in both of his letters to Timothy to encourage and direct him in this matter. This is particularly evident in the focus text above, where Paul instructs Timothy to fix his attention continuously on the eternal Scriptures instead of getting misled by the popular "teachings" of that moment. He tells Timothy that God's Word will be the tool that keeps him on track even as others get derailed. It will equip Timothy to minister to others as he teaches doctrines, rebukes heresies, corrects sin and faulty teachings, and trains the church for holy living (2 Timothy 3:16).

ALL SCRIPTURE IS INSPIRED BY GOD

We will never run to the Scriptures as our number one ministry tool unless in the depths of our souls we believe it is the inspired Word of God. Only when we acknowledge God's authoritative voice in its pages will his truths complete and equip us for all aspects of ministry. John Ellicott in his *Commentary for English Readers* says of the inspired Word:

> From it [the servant of God] must prove the doctrines he professes; hence, too, he must draw his reproofs for the ignorant and erring. It must be the one source whence he derives those instructions which teach the Christian how to grow in grace.
>
> —John Ellicott

If the Scriptures are to be the single voice above all others that guides our life and ministry, then we must be thoroughly convinced we are building upon a sure foundation. To reach this conclusion with integrity, we need to ask, "Is it true that God communicated his mind to us through the personalities and creative genius of the biblical writers?"

At a foundational level, our ministry and faith really come down to how this question is answered. Many well-meaning Christians point to Bible verses that clearly say the Scriptures are inspired by God. I'd love to say, "Problem solved!" But this hasn't really settled the issue because using these verses as a proof-text is only helpful if you've started with the presupposition that the verses themselves are inspired. Any text can self-proclaim that its origins are from God, and in fact many false religious documents do just that.

So if we can't use the Bible to prove its own inspiration, how do we prove it? The only honest answer is that we can't. At least not in the systematic method we would with a scientific theory. We can show historically how the biblical texts came to be considered Scripture and how their textual integrity has been preserved over the centuries. But we can't do the same thing for proving their inspiration. For that, the burden of proof has to come from a combination of faith and experience. Christian author and pastor John Piper writes:

> There is a divine glory that shines through [scripture], which fits perfectly with the God-shaped template in your heart—like sprocket and gear, hand and glove, fish and water, wings and air, the final piece of a jigsaw puzzle.[1]
>
> —John Piper

Piper's thoughts on this matter reflect David's heart when he wrote Psalm 19, a beautiful song that gives witness to the life-altering power of Scripture. Among its imagery, David writes that the Word of God:

> Is perfect, refreshing the soul . . . trustworthy, making wise the simple . . . right, giving joy to the heart . . . radiant, giving light to the eyes . . . more precious than gold . . . sweeter than honey, than honey from the honeycomb.
>
> —Psalm 19:7-10, NIV

What David has expressed through this poetic imagery is that when God is at work in us, his words make our souls come to life. When that happens, we are convinced that we've been touched by the very breath of God.

REFLECT AND APPLY

How convinced are you that God communicated his mind to us through the personalities and creative genius of the biblical writers? When have you experienced Scripture in the same way that David wrote of in the Psalm 19 prayer at the start of the chapter?

CHAPTER TWENTY-FIVE
PROFITABLE FOR TEACHING DOCTRINE

All scripture is inspired by God, and profitable for teaching, for rebuking, for correcting, for training in righteousness, so that the man of God may be complete, equipped for every good work.

—*2 Timothy 3:16*

ON OCTOBER 31, 1517, GERMAN PRIEST Martin Luther nailed his 95 Theses to the door of the castle church in the small town of Wittenberg, eastern Germany, kicking off the Reformation. Luther's overwhelming desire to put God's Word into the hands of the common man saw him translating the Latin New Testament into the German vernacular as well as writing many books and sermons for the edification of the church. So imagine his surprise when he discovered a little over a decade later that church members in his parishes were ignorant of the most basic biblical doctrines. After this discovery, he wrote:

> The deplorable, miserable conditions which I recently observed when visiting parishes have constrained and pressed me to put this catechism of Christian Doctrine into brief, plain, and simple form. How pitiable, so help me God, were the things I saw: the common man, especially in the villages, knows practically nothing of Christian doctrine, and many of the pastors are almost entirely incompetent and unable to teach.[1]
>
> —Martin Luther

Luther's response to this discouraging situation was to write *The Small Catechism*, which included the Lord's Prayer, the Apostle's Creed, and the Ten Commandments. He created this simple teaching tool for pastors and parents because the commoners of this time were functionally illiterate. Through explanation, repetition, and memorization of key Bible passages and doctrines, Luther believed he could inform and transform the biblically ignorant Christians of his day.

ORAL METHODS FOR TEACHING BIBLICAL DOCTRINE

Five centuries later, we find ourselves in a situation very similar to Luther's. The International Orality Network estimates that 5.7 billion of the world's 7.8 billion people more easily process information orally rather than in written form.[2] By my estimations, that's roughly three quarters of the world's population.

This helps explain why even where believers have access to a wide variety of Bibles and Christian books in their mother tongue, the average church member remains biblically and doctrinally ignorant. The solution to this problem can't just be more doctrinal books that gather dust. Rather, pastors and church leaders need to rediscover the appropriateness of teaching biblical doctrines through oral methods like creeds, catechisms, and biblically based songs.

Many modern Christians, especially in the industrialized world, associate such oral methods with "high church" religion and consider them better left to our liturgical past. But that mindset is a form of "chronological snobbery," a term C. S. Lewis used in his book *Surprised by Joy* to describe the tendency of each new generation to disregard as dated and irrelevant the wisdom of the past. Instead of dismissing these great guardians of truth, we must breathe new life into them by couching them in the biblical stories from which they came. By allowing them to flow from their proper context, we will give them back their ability to excite and transform.

When I came to this realization as a young ministry leader, I was very interested in learning how to share the truths of God's written Word in a way that could be accessible to a primarily oral world. As it turns out, this looks similar to a young Jewish rabbi telling stories in the Galilean countryside. While Jesus made this look easy, it took me some training to get back to my own oral roots. Part of this process involved learning storytelling techniques from a missionary who was sharing the truths of God's Word through Bible stories and indigenous music. The month I spent with him along the northern border of Uganda, East Africa, was a powerful lesson in orality and reproducibility.

We would arrive at a village after a long hike, where my job was to crank a hand-held tape recorder, announcing our presence. If I cranked hard enough, a steady stream of Bible stories set to music would draw in the men, women, and children. As they joined their voices with the recorded music, the men would lean their bows, spears, and guns against the "story tree." After everyone settled down, the missionary would ask someone to review last week's Bible story, then he would tell a new one. This was no solemn affair as the locals always helped in retelling the story and would often act out the biblical scenes with plenty of energy and laughter.

On one of these occasions, we showed up to a village only to find they were in the middle of a wedding celebration. Noticing that everyone had already started dipping into their local beer, made from a grain called sorghum, we politely suggested we save our story for the next visit. They would have none of it, insisting we share a story from God's Word. After a brief discussion, my colleague and I decided there was only one obvious choice. So the missionary told the story where Jesus turns the water into wine at the wedding in Cana (John 2:1-12). When he finished, the missionary asked, "What does this story teach us about Jesus?"

The villagers discussed this with each other for a long time before giving an answer. Finally, they responded, "It tells us that if Jesus can change something in creation into something else, then that means he must be the creator. And if he is the creator, then that can only mean he is God."

I will never forget seeing the spiritual light within their hearts turn on. In that moment, the Holy Spirit revealed to them a Christological doctrine that took the early church two hundred years and the Council of Nicaea to agree upon.

This experience and others like it have shown me that we can teach the doctrines of our faith through the stories we find in God's Word. While the Reformation has rightly put God's Word back into the hands of the common man, it would still serve us well to interact with it in tandem with other external doctrinal resources like creeds and catechisms. It is important to realize that the Scriptures and doctrinal confessions are not mutually exclusive.

Yes, we must be careful to avoid giving these tools equal weight with the Scriptures or using them to interpret the Scriptures. But when we use them as guard rails along the path of personal Bible memorization, study, and teaching, they can keep us from wandering off into heresy. As spiritual leaders who stand watch over our families and faith communities, it falls on us to teach them clear confessions that will guard against heresies and guide them through their discovery of God's Word, oral or written.

Public Worship and Common Prayer

Just as I've become an advocate of breathing new life into the classic oral teaching methods of the church, I've also come to value the way liturgy can take the truths of God's Word from a person's head to their heart. Though the word *liturgy* can sound old-fashioned, it simply means public worship. For many contemporary churches, the term public worship can often mean coming together to observe a worship service that primarily happens on a stage. Other than joining in the singing and contributing to the offering plate, little is expected in the way of participation.

One way to guard against making the corporate church experience one of passive entertainment is to incorporate liturgical principles into the service. True to its meaning of public worship, liturgy plans for the whole congregation to participate in activities that include praise, thanksgiving, remembrance, supplication, and repentance. All congregants are expected to physically and verbally respond to God's Word and presence.

My first experience with a liturgical service was at a Lutheran church in East Africa. I was impressed with how every part of the service was purposefully centered around one clear biblical theme. From the prayers to the songs to the homily (or short sermon), a distinct biblical truth was continually being revisited and therefore reinforced. This was because the order of the service, and in fact the services for the whole year, came from their liturgy and lectionary (a yearly biblical reading plan).

The second thing that impressed me was my participation in the service. I was expected to recite creeds, stand for the Scripture reading, sing worship songs, participate in call and response prayers, give testimony for God's faithfulness, and walk up to receive the Lord's Supper from the pastor. My time with them that morning was more than just a worship service that I attended but rather a corporate experience of worship in which I took part. And although their expression of God's universal church isn't the only way to do corporate worship, there was much about that service to be appreciated and emulated.

REFLECT AND APPLY

Based on whether you are an oral or visual learner, what liturgical tools can you use as guide rails in your faith?

CHAPTER TWENTY-SIX
PROFITABLE FOR REBUKING AND CORRECTING

All scripture is inspired by God, and profitable for teaching, for rebuking, for correcting, for training in righteousness, so that the man of God may be complete, equipped for every good work.

—2 Timothy 3:16

BECAUSE THE TOPICS OF REBUKING AND CORRECTING often overlap each other, I will address them both in this chapter. When we approach the topic of church discipline, it is important to understand that as God's servants, our authority to correct, discipline, and condemn only extends to those who claim to be believers. Or as 1 Corinthians 5:11 says, "Anyone who bears the name of brother." While there is a place to confront sin in the world, those outside the church are not under our jurisdiction, nor should we expect them to play by our rules (1 Corinthians 5:9-10). But inside the church, we are required to correct unrepentant sin and wrong teachings as well as rebuke heresies.

We need to make sure we don't confuse correcting and rebuking because each is meant to lead to a very different outcome. We gently correct habitual sin and faulty teachings with a goal of repentance and reconciliation. In contrast, we strongly rebuke heresies to preserve the truth and unity in our communities. In this chapter, we will look at when each of these is appropriate as well as how to go about them scripturally.

CONFRONTING UNREPENTANT SIN

The apostle Paul tells us in his first epistle to the Corinthian church that we must keep our distance from those claiming to be believers but who are living in blatant, unrepentant sin against God and his Word. In fact, he adds that we shouldn't even meet up with them "for coffee or tea."

But now I am writing to you not to associate with anyone who bears the name of brother if he is guilty of sexual immorality or greed, or is an idolater, reviler, drunkard, or swindler—not even to eat with such a one.

—1 Corinthians 5:11

While totally disassociating from such believers may seem harsh, it is needed so they don't infect the rest of the church body. In the medical world, a doctor will do all that is necessary to save an infected limb. But if at some point it becomes evident the infected limb will endanger the health of the entire body, a decision to amputate must be made. Like a doctor, pastors and church leaders must have as their goal the restoration of a damaged church member, but when it becomes evident restoration is no longer possible, they must be cut off for the health of the body. Jesus himself gave us the pattern for dealing with sinful behavior in the church.

If your brother sins against you, go and tell him his fault, between you and him alone. If he listens to you, you have gained your brother. But if he does not listen, take one or two others along with you, that every charge may be established by the evidence of two or three witnesses. If he refuses to listen to them, tell it to the church. And if he refuses to listen even to the church, let him be to you as a Gentile and a tax collector.

—Matthew 18: 15-17

Notice that the first response for a personal offense should be to correct the person in private. If they repent and make things right, the goal of restoration is accomplished. If they refuse, we are to try again, this time bringing along a couple of other people who are aware of the situation. If this doesn't work, the situation must be taken to the church.

This final step is important. It isn't for the pastor or a single church leader to deal with unrepentant sin alone. The situation is to be taken to the church elders so that it can be dealt with collectively under the power, authority, and guidance of the Holy Spirit.

Only when the unrepentant person refuses to listen to the highest authority of the church is complete disassociation deemed necessary. And even then, this "sanctified shunning" isn't carried out maliciously but with the intent of keeping the rest of the church pure while simultaneously giving the sinner space for repentance. Mandatory social disassociation from the faith community lets people know they have to make a choice to follow God or walk away from him. It's a reminder to them and the rest of the church that believers can't live in Christian community and willfully live in sin.

Correcting Wrong Teaching

It is only natural for people in our congregations to have faulty theology. None of us are born into God's kingdom with a perfect understanding of his truths. The perfecting of our faith and theology is a lifelong process that only ends when we see Jesus face to face. So when we bump up against well-meaning but faulty teachings in others, let's be slow to cry heresy but fast to address it. As uncomfortable as this may be, it will save the teacher and their students from drifting away from sound biblical truths as faulty teaching can become false teaching if not dealt with quickly and appropriately.

As Paul instructed Timothy, the faulty teacher should neither be attacked or ignored but approached humbly as "a father, younger men as brothers, older women as mothers, younger women as sisters, in all purity" (1 Timothy 5:1-2).

This means speaking gently in ways that protect their dignity while being clear where we perceive them to be in error. It is always profitable to start such an encounter with a prayer, asking for the Holy Spirit's presence and insight, then with humility study the contested Scripture passage together. By doing this, you ensure that this "error" is not a matter of your convictions against theirs but that both of you are under the submission of God's Word.

This approach has the added benefit of modeling how to handle Scripture, which will lessen the likelihood of needing to confront this person's teaching again. If after studying God's Word together, there is still no unity over the contested teaching, the matter should be brought before the elders of the church for their guidance and instruction.

A common mistake in the church, especially at the small group level, is for teachers to present their own personal convictions as biblical truths. The Bible has many clear dos and don'ts in it. But because the gospel is more about heart transformation and principles than outwardly obeying detailed rules, there is a lot of room for people to differ on how they live out their faith.

The apostle Paul addressed the early church repeatedly on this topic, telling believers to respect each other's differing convictions on peripheral matters (Romans 14; 1 Corinthians 8). He addressed most strongly quarrels over which day to worship on or restrictions on what to eat or drink. He doesn't say it's wrong to have these different convictions, only that it's wrong to impose them on others as God's decree.

> Therefore let no one pass judgment on you in questions of food and drink, or with regard to a festival or a new moon or a Sabbath. These are a shadow of the things to come, but the substance belongs to Christ. Let no one disqualify you, insisting on asceticism and worship of angels, going on in detail about visions, puffed up without reason by his sensuous mind, and not holding fast to the Head, from whom the whole body, nourished and knit together through its joints and ligaments, grows with a growth that is from God.
>
> —Colossians 2:16-19

When teachers become extra-biblical and impose their own standards on clothes, alcohol, types of education, or styles of worship and music, they have strayed into legalism, and their teachings become divisive. Paul describes these people as "puffed up without reason" (v. 18), who have lost their perspective in Christ and need help getting their focus back on him.

An example of legalistic teachings that bring division in the church is a situation that arose in the late second century over when Christians should celebrate Easter. Up to this point in church history, the churches of Asia Minor always celebrated Easter on the date of the Jewish Passover. The rest of Christianity celebrated it on a Sunday even if the date didn't line up with the Passover.

This wasn't an issue until Pope Victor (known then as the fourteenth Bishop of Rome) decided it was high time to unite Christianity on this matter. In an effort to do this, he declared that all believers needed to follow the Sunday-only tradition. When the churches in Asia Minor refused to obey this edict, the infuriated pope proceeded to excommunicate all believers who would not change their stance.

Thankfully, the great peacemaker and church father, Irenaeus, was able to talk some sense into Pope Victor by reminding him that Pope Anacletus (third Bishop of Rome) and St. Polycarp faced this same issue a full century earlier but were able to preserve their friendship. Because of Irenaeus's correction, Pope Victor backed down on the issue. In this way, Irenaeus was able to preserve the peace and guard the church against the faulty teaching of Pope Victor.[1]

REBUKING HERESY

The unbelieving world says all manner of false things about God and his Word. While their Creator will hold them accountable for every word that comes out of their mouths, these people are not heretics. Only those who claim to be Christians can commit heresy. That is because the accusation of heresy is reserved for those who try to distort the very truth of God's Word, which they claim to follow. Like Satan, who pretends to be an angel of light, they disguise themselves as God's servants while they spread their lies against him.

> For such men are false apostles, deceitful workmen, disguising themselves
> as apostles of Christ. And no wonder, for even Satan disguises himself as
> an angel of light. So it is no surprise if his servants, also, disguise

themselves as servants of righteousness. Their end will correspond to their deeds.

—2 Corinthians 11:13-15

Nineteenth-century theologian Friedrich Schleiermacher described heresy as "that which preserved the appearance of Christianity, and yet contradicted its essence." Paul described such people as "having the appearance of godliness, but denying its power" (2 Timothy 3:5).

While correcting sin and faulty teaching is done with gentleness, rebuking heresy needs to be a firm, no-nonsense exercise. This isn't interacting with a well-meaning teacher who has misinterpreted a Bible passage by accident. This is someone deliberately deceiving the flock and taking advantage of the weak for personal gain, power, and/or prestige. With people like this, there is only one course of action to protect the spiritual life of the church. That is to go to war with them and their false teachings.

One man who knew what it meant to take extreme action against heresy was the early church father Athanasius of Alexandria. He earned his nickname "God's hammer" when he spent most of his life beating down the false teachings of Arianism. Athanasius's ability to detect and defend against heresy came from all the time he spent in God's Word. St Gregory of Nazingnus said at Athanasius's funeral that Athanasius "meditated on every book of the Old and New Testament with a depth as such as none has applied even to one of them."[2] His understanding of Scripture guided the church through some very formative days as they were trying to figure out important doctrines concerning Jesus and the Trinity. Because of his efforts, heresies that could have fractured the church became opportunities to unite it in orthodoxy.

Paul gave the servants of God a clear and concise battle plan to use against heresy when he wrote to another young ministry leader and protégé, Titus.

> But avoid foolish controversies, genealogies, dissensions, and quarrels about the law, for they are unprofitable and worthless. As for a person who stirs up division, after warning him once and then twice, have nothing more to do with him, knowing that such a person is warped and sinful; he is self-condemned.
>
> —Titus 3:9-11

Notice that phase one is to avoid being drawn into divisive debates about pointless words and theories. Engaging in this fruitless activity only makes you a part of the problem. Instead, shut it down and bring your congregation back to the core truths of the gospel. Phase two is to warn the false teacher to stop causing disunity through his teachings. If they continue in their rebellion even after two warnings, the elders of the church must move to phase three, which is to cast these false teachers out of the faith community.

This is a full excommunication, which means they are rejected from the community, delivered to Satan for punishment, and they bring a curse on themselves (1 Corinthians 5:5). This may seem extreme, but we must remember that this is a spiritual battle being waged against the life of the congregation.

REFLECT AND APPLY

As you sit under others' teachings, how can you tell the difference between a faulty teaching and a false teaching?

CHAPTER TWENTY-SEVEN
PROFITABLE FOR TRAINING IN RIGHTEOUSNESS

All scripture is inspired by God, and profitable for teaching, for rebuking, for correcting, for training in righteousness, so that the man of God may be complete, equipped for every good work.

—*2 Timothy 3:16*

But as for you, continue in what you have learned and firmly believed. You know those who taught you, and you know that from childhood you have known the sacred Scriptures, which are able to give you wisdom for salvation through faith in Christ Jesus.

—*1 Timothy 3:14-15*

THERE IS ONE COMMONLY MISINTERPRETED Bible verse from the apostle Paul's epistles that people love to apply to just about any challenge they face in life: "I can do all things through Christ who strengthens me" (Philippians 4:13).

While this verse may give us the emotional boost we are looking for to pass the big exam or become top salesperson in our department, that isn't what Paul's statement is about. Jesus Christ is not a motivational speaker just waiting to give us the confidence we need to attain all of our personal goals. Paul wrote this epistle while under house arrest. Continuing on from the prior passage we looked at (Philippians 4:11-12), Paul was expressing his ability through Christ to be content in all the difficult situations he'd mentioned, whether hungry or full, locked-up or free. So a more correct application of this passage would be to say, "Pass or fail, top salesperson or not, I can be content in Christ who strengthens me."

As you can see, how we interpret God's Word drastically changes how we apply it to our lives. When Paul speaks of the Scriptures as being profitable for "training in righteousness" (2 Timothy 3:16), he is referring to the application of righteousness in our daily lives. And part of that application process is first knowing how to interpret it.

I thank God there are many excellent tools like Bible dictionaries, lexicons, and commentaries that can aid us at times in doing this more effectively. But it is also good to keep in mind some basic principles that, applied properly, can enable us to navigate most of what we find in the Bible. As such, I would strongly suggest starting with these principles and only using Bible study aids when extra support is needed.

PRINCIPLE #1: WE CAN ONLY UNDERSTAND GOD'S THOUGHTS THROUGH HIS SPIRIT

In the gospel of John, we see Jesus perform seven miracles or signs intended to show that he came from God and that the things he said about himself were true. The typical response of religious leaders to these signs was to ignore them and react instead against the claims Jesus made about himself, usually because these claims strongly hinted at his deity. This pattern came to a breaking point when Jesus brought his friend Lazarus back from the dead (John 11). Before Jesus performed what would be his last and greatest sign, he made one more claim.

> I am the resurrection and the life. Whoever believes in me, though he die,
> yet shall he live, and everyone who lives and believes in me shall never die.
>
> —John 11:25

This claim and the sign that went with it were what finally pushed the religious establishment over the edge to begin plotting the murder of their Messiah and Savior of the world. Their response to Jesus is summed up by the ruling high priest Caiaphas, who told his fellow religious rulers:

> You know nothing at all, nor do you understand that it is better for you
> that one man should die for the people, not that the whole nation should
> perish.
>
> —John 11:50

225

How was it possible that these religious leaders who had studied and memorized the entire Old Testament could not see the Word of God standing in their midst? According to the apostle Paul, there was, in fact, no way these men could perceive the mysteries of God because they were leaning on their own understanding while God's mysteries can only be perceived through the Holy Spirit.

> But we impart a secret and hidden wisdom of God, which God decreed before the ages for our glory. None of the rulers of this age understood this, for if they had, they would not have crucified the Lord of glory. But, as it is written, "What no eye has seen, no ear heard, nor the heart of man imagined, what God has prepared for those who love him"—these things God has revealed to us through the Spirit. For the Spirit searches everything, even the depths of God. For who knows a person's thoughts except the spirit of that person, which is in him? So also no one comprehends the thoughts of God except the Spirit of God. Now we have received not the spirit of the world, but the Spirit who is from God, that we might understand the things freely given us by God.
>
> —1 Corinthians 2:7-12

This passage is a good reminder that no matter how much biblical knowledge we have, we can't understand God's thoughts without the help of the Holy Spirit because only the Holy Spirit is able to perceive the mind of God. Someone whose understanding comes from "the spirit of this world" (v. 12) and someone whose understanding comes from "the Spirit who is from God" can look at the same passage of Scripture and walk away with diametrically opposed interpretations.

God gave us his Spirit so "that we might understand the things freely given us" (v. 12). This is why it is vital that we go to God's Word hand-in-hand with the Holy Spirit so he can help us understand the mind of God found in its pages.

PRINCIPLE #2: WE COME TO THE SCRIPTURES TO FIND GOD'S TRUTH, NOT OURS

Along with going to God's Word under the Holy Spirit's tutelage, we also need to approach with a humble learner's attitude. Practically speaking, just what does a learner's attitude look like? The apostle James tells us that it starts with listening.

> Know this, my beloved brothers: let every person be quick to hear, slow to speak, slow to anger; for the anger of man does not produce the righteousness of God. Therefore put away all filthiness and rampant wickedness and receive with meekness the implanted word, which is able to save your souls.
>
> —James 1:19-20

Having open ears and a closed mouth is a posture that shows our desire is to understand. This goes against our natural desire of wanting others to understand and affirm us. But when being understood is our top priority, our minds and mouths are full of our own ideas, and little learning is able to happen. As we come to God's Word, it is crucial we check our impulse to impose our opinions and ideas onto it instead allowing God's truths to speak for themselves.

And they are speaking. The question is whether we are listening. Or are we too busy looking for ways to justify our points of view and life choices?

We have to ask these questions of ourselves because if we don't go to the Scriptures with a learner's attitude, it's a very easy jump into dangerous territory. All it takes is bending one obscure verse out of context to manipulate the Bible to say whatever we want. This is how most heresies and cults start. If we are more interested in God changing us than we are in trying to change God, we must go to the Scriptures humbly and "receive with meekness the implanted word, which is able to save [our] souls" (James 1:20).

PRINCIPLE #3: GETTING AN APPROPRIATE APPLICATION STARTS WITH ASKING THE RIGHT QUESTION

As we interact with the Bible's eternal truths, we will notice that it is packed full of commands, stories, poems, letters, and prophecies written over thousands of years. How do we navigate all of that and know what applies to us today? This process can be complicated, but it usually comes down to asking a simple question: "Is the passage we're reading descriptive or prescriptive?"

A *descriptive passage* narrates an event that has taken place but doesn't give a command to follow. The book of Judges is a good example of this. It describes how God used broken people in a dark period of Israel's history. The point of Judges was to show humanity's depravity when they walked away from God, not to condone or encourage the judges' often shameful behavior. While many life principles can be learned from descriptive passages, they were mainly written to reveal truths about God and how he has ordered our world.

Prescriptive passages, much like a medical prescription, have an expectation that we will apply them to our lives. They often show up in the form of Judaic laws in the Old Testament or instructions to the church in the New Testament. The key to prescriptive passages is to find out if they are specific to the original readers or if they are commands that can and should be transferred to believers of every time and culture. To do this, one needs a good understanding of the context of the passage, both historically and textually.

An example of this is the commandment given to Israel on Mt. Sinai: "You shall not murder." Although this and the other Ten Commandments (Exodus 20:1-17) were given specifically to the nation of Israel at a unique time in their history, this command is repeated throughout the Bible at different times and in different ways. In his Sermon on the Mount, Jesus gave an even fuller application to our lives.

> You have heard that it was said to those of old, "You shall not murder; and whoever murders will be liable to judgment." But I say to you that everyone who is angry with his brother will be liable to judgment.
>
> —Matthew 5:21-22a

Because this command is reiterated throughout Scripture, we can be confident that "you shall not murder" is a command to be obeyed by all people in every generation. When trying to live out the gospel, knowing the difference between descriptive and prescriptive passages will be one of the best guides to help us in its interpretation and application.

PRINCIPLE #4: WE MUST BE DOERS OF GOD'S WORD AND NOT JUST HEARERS IF WE WANT A BLESSING

Up to this point in the chapter, we've been talking about how to understand the Bible and apply it to our lives. But our next step is obedience. After telling us to have open ears and a closed mouth, the apostle James goes on to say that we can't just stop at listening but must go on to actually act on God's Word.

> But be doers of the word, and not hearers only, deceiving yourselves. For if anyone is a hearer of the word and not a doer, he is like a man who looks intently at his natural face in a mirror. For he looks at himself and goes away and at once forgets what he was like. But the one who looks into the perfect law, the law of liberty, and perseveres, being no hearer who forgets but a doer who acts, he will be blessed in his doing.
>
> —James 1:22-25

Learning and application are connected to each other fundamentally, and they only make sense if they are kept together. You can't apply what you haven't learned. And what would be the point in learning something you have no intention of applying? For example, what would be the point in paying money to attend a workshop on how to eat healthy, then picking up a large burger, fries, and milkshake on the way home? Or why attend a lecture to hear someone's expertise on a subject and not take notes so you can ponder and apply what they said later?

In the passage above, James asks basically the same question. Why even go to a mirror to look at yourself if you're not planning on doing anything to change your appearance? It's a poor use of your time and a wasted opportunity to make yourself look more presentable. James connects this kind of foolishness to interacting with God's Word. When we go to its pages, our goal shouldn't just be to understand its truths but to instantly apply them to our lives in practical and tangible ways. Anything less than that is just plain foolishness.

Yet that is what so many believers do each week when they go to church. They hear God's Word preached, intellectually acknowledge a "powerful truth," then walk away forgetting that they need to apply it to their own life. They think that just because they "looked in the mirror," they are somehow magically presentable before God. As James says, this is very self-deceptive because there is no blessing in hearing God's Word unless it causes us to change.

PRINCIPLE #5: DON'T GET DISTRACTED WITH BOOKS ABOUT THE BIBLE ABOVE THE BIBLE ITSELF

One important final caution is not to get so caught up in reading about the Bible that you actually stop reading the Bible itself. King Solomon once stated: "Of making many books there is no end" (Ecclesiastes 12:12). This is a truism for all books, including devotionals, theological writings, and the Christian self-help genre.

There are so many good spiritual books available but only one perfect book that comes from the mind of God. We would do well to give that book the bulk of our time and attention since it is the Scriptures that bring us to Christ, and it will be the Scriptures that keep us coming back to him. Like the church of Ephesus, much of the modern church is distracted and chasing after new and exciting teachings. Paul tells us that the only way to avoid joining this trend is to stay on focused in the Scriptures themselves.

This could be any combination of daily Scripture readings, in-depth Bible studies, times of reflection, and memorization of Scripture (verse by verse or by oral Bible stories). Although different cultures will tend to focus on some of these more than others, all have their place and are valuable in keeping our hearts and minds grounded on the kingdom of God.

This is an apt word for the messages we preach to others and for the ones we need to preach to ourselves. As Paul reminded Timothy, only inasmuch as God's followers saturate themselves in God's Word will we be complete in our faith and equipped for every good work that God calls us to do (2 Timothy 3:16).

Reflect and Apply

How have you approached Scripture in the past? After reading this chapter, is there anything that will change as you approach Scripture in the future?

GOING DEEPER

SUGGESTED ACTIVITIES

1. Pick a book of the Bible and do an in-depth study on it, implementing what you have learned from this section.

2. If you don't come from a liturgical background, choose a week to visit a church that uses liturgy throughout its service. Reflect on what you found beneficial that could enhance your own faith tradition.

3. Memorize one or all of the following: the Lord's Prayer, the Apostle's Creed, and the Ten Commandments.

4. Research a heresy of the early church. Find out why it was considered a heresy, who were the major players on each side, and how it was resolved.

SUGGESTED READING:

Living By The Book by Howard G. Hendricks and William D. Hendricks

Common Prayer: A Liturgy for Ordinary Radicals by Shane Claiborne, Jonathan Wilson-Hartgrove, and Enuma Okoro

SECTION EIGHT:
FULFILLING OUR MINISTRY TO GOD

It is truly good and right for us to pray to your majesty, that when our Lord comes, he will find us serving our coworkers. In our dealings with your people, help us to be careful to balance affection with correction and needful rebukes with love, that we wisely discharge the service committed to us and not become guilty of failing to put our Lord's deposit to work but profit from having multiplied God's talents of which we have been made the stewards.

—Leo 1

Bishop of Rome, fourth century

CHAPTER TWENTY-EIGHT
A RESPONSIBILITY OF STEWARDSHIP

I solemnly charge you before God and Christ Jesus, who is going to judge the living and the dead, and because of His appearing and His Kingdom. Proclaim the message; persist in it whether convenient or not; rebuke, correct, and encourage with great patience and teaching.

—2 Timothy 4:1-2

But I do not account my life of any value nor as precious to myself, if only I may finish my course and the ministry that I received from the Lord Jesus, to testify to the gospel of the grace of God.

—Acts 20:24

AFTER SERVING IN CROSS-CULTURAL MINISTRY for six years in Tanzania, East Africa, I accepted a leadership position with the same organization. This involved providing oversight to missionary teams all over Africa. My predecessor briefed me on my new ministry role, gave me a company laptop, then showed me to my office. Not only was this my first official office, but it came with a door I could shut at will, a luxury after living communally in a small village. Things were looking good.

But just before walking out my new door, my predecessor informed me: "By the way, the first thing you'll need to do is call this particular person and tell them that because of their ongoing failure to submit to leadership, they'll need to leave their team and go home. After that, you may need to travel to their ministry location and address other dysfunctional problems that are threatening to destroy the team."

With that, he closed the door to both my office and any notion that my new position would be convenient or stress-free. That said, it still ended up being one of the most fulfilling ministry experiences I've ever had.

OUR REASONS FOR SERVING GOD

A transition from the romantic idealism of a new ministry opportunity to the reality of what it fully entails is bound to happen. Maybe not as quickly as in the above situation, but it will come. I don't say this to discourage those being led into ministry opportunities or even to commiserate with my "fellows in the trenches," but because it is important to consider just why we serve.

Yes, serving in a ministry can be very rewarding. But if motivations are primarily about personal fulfillment, we will find ourselves frequently disappointed and tempted to quit when things get hard or we no longer feel valued. Serving our Lord is a blessing. But it also comes with an expectation that we will faithfully steward what God has entrusted to us regardless of the challenges.

In 2 Timothy, we see Timothy's mentor Paul walking out the door of his life and into the hereafter. This wasn't what Timothy signed up for when he joined Paul's ministry. Gone were the exciting days when he and Paul traveled the known world, planting churches for Jesus. Timothy was now stationed at Ephesus without Paul, trying to battle heretics and provide leadership to a church that was going through a tumultuous time. It's quite possible Timothy would have been tempted to abandon his responsibilities since the church was not valuing his leadership position.

What Timothy needed was motivation and focus. Paul gave him a hefty dose of both by reminding him of his duty to minister to this dysfunctional church even if they weren't receptive to his efforts (see 2 Timothy 4:1-2 above). Unlike today's popular motivational speakers, Paul said nothing to Timothy about feeling good about himself if he persevered in his efforts. Nor did he promise: "This too shall pass."

Instead, Paul tells Timothy that the reason he must stay the course is because he will have to give an account when Jesus comes back on how he led this church. This sobering reminder of eternal accountability comes from Paul's deep sense of responsibility to God for his own ministry. To Paul, completing the ministry he'd received from God was a matter of obedience and stewardship.

FULFILLING OUR MINISTRIES REQUIRES OBEDIENCE AND STEWARDSHIP

In Acts 20, we see this strong conviction spill out during Paul's farewell speech to the elders of Ephesus. Knowing he will be arrested in Jerusalem and will never again see these men, Paul begins his farewell address by affirming that he has fulfilled his ministry to the Ephesian church.

> You yourselves know how I lived among you the whole time from the first day that I set foot in Asia, serving the Lord with all humility and with tears and with trials that happened to me through the plots of the Jews; how I did not shrink from declaring to you anything that was profitable, and teaching you in public and from house to house, testifying both to Jews and to Greeks of repentance toward God and of faith in our Lord Jesus Christ.
>
> —Acts 20:18-21

The format Paul uses in his goodbye speech is one seen in other biblical farewells, including Moses (Deuteronomy 31), Samuel (1 Samuel 12), and Jesus (Luke 22). Each started out with a declaration of having fulfilled their responsibilities in life and ministry. In Paul's own farewell speech, he was able to say with confidence that he had not "shrunk back" from ministering to the Ephesian believers despite many hardships. Even as plots were hatched against him by his enemies, he'd persisted in his call by teaching them the Scriptures and proclaiming the Good News of Jesus to the lost in their city. Paul felt the weight of fulfilling his ministry towards them so much that later in his speech he emphasized:

> I count my life of no value to myself, so that I may finish my course and the ministry I received from the Lord Jesus to testify to the gospel of God's grace.
>
> —Acts 20:24, HCSB

Paul's ministry to the church of Ephesus was to proclaim the gospel of Christ to them, and he never allowed trials or oppositions to stop him from doing that. This was the deep sense of sacrificial ministry he longed for Timothy to have towards this church. He wanted Timothy to view his role at Ephesus, not as a job posting to be endured or abandoned, but as a ministry entrusted to him by God to fulfill.

This is my desire for each of you reading this book. My hope and prayer is that someday when you are giving your own farewell address to those whom you are currently serving, you will be able to deliver the "fulfillment of ministry" section with a humble confidence as Paul did.

REFLECT AND APPLY

How does viewing your job as a position that God has entrusted you to fulfill, not as something that can be endured or abandoned, transform your attitude towards work?

CHAPTER TWENTY-NINE
GETTING SERIOUS ABOUT SERVICE

For the time will come when they will not tolerate sound doctrine, but according to their own desires, will multiply teachers for themselves because they have an itch to hear something new. They will turn away from hearing the truth and will turn aside to myths. But as for you, be serious about everything, endure hardship, do the work of an evangelist, fulfill your ministry.

—2 Timothy 4:3-5 (HCSB)

PAUL DOESN'T STOP WITH SOLEMNLY CHARGING Timothy to stay the course in his ministry. He goes on to provide Timothy with a ministry fulfillment checklist (v. 5 above). Notice that Paul mentions four specific items on this checklist.

- Be serious about everything.
- Endure hardship.
- Do the work of an evangelist.
- Fulfill your ministry.

We will unpack each of these checklist items over the next chapters, beginning with the first: "Be serious about everything." A common problem for people who are serious about serving God is that they can also take themselves too seriously. I've often been guilty of confusing seriousness with godliness. Because of this, God has given me a wife who loves to have fun. She is a gift of joy, and her presence reminds me that laughter is from God and should have a prominent place in every balanced life.

So if joy and laughter are such good things, why does Paul say we need to be serious (or sober/sober-minded/vigilant in other translations) about everything? Did he like myself need to loosen up a little? Perhaps. But when we look at how Paul uses the same original Greek word in some of his other epistles, we see that he isn't referring to seriousness of temperament but a serious intentionality to stay alert. So in the context of this letter, we understand that Paul isn't telling Timothy to be a somber, humorless minister, but to stay alert as he awaits Christ's return, particularly against false teachers and heresies.

GETTING SERIOUS ABOUT STAYING ALERT

We see this same idea of intentional alertness in Paul's epistle to the church of Thessalonica as he exhorts them to stay vigilant in their faith and love because in the last days people will be lulled to sleep spiritually by a false sense of security.

> While people are saying, "There is peace and security," then sudden destruction will come upon them as labor pains come upon a pregnant woman, and they will not escape. But you are not in darkness, brothers, for that day to surprise you like a thief. For you are all children of light, children of the day. We are not of the night or of the darkness. So then let us not sleep, as others do, but **let us keep awake and be sober.** For those who sleep, sleep at night, and those who get drunk, are drunk at night. But since we belong to the day, let us be sober, having put on the breastplate of faith and love, and for a helmet the hope of salvation. (emphasis mine)
>
> —1 Thessalonians 5:3-8

A pregnant woman isn't surprised that she will give birth to a baby at some point. All the signs in her body point to this fact. The surprise is when a pregnant woman goes to sleep assured she still has weeks to her due date but is caught unprepared in the middle of the night with labor pains and no midwife contacted or bags packed for the hospital.

This is how it will be in the last days for even some who call themselves Christians but are caught spiritually sleeping. They will find themselves unprepared because they have been deceived by false teachings promising peace and security. This was the same warning Paul gave to Timothy when he challenged him to be serious about staying alert. Why? Because people will stop tolerating sound doctrine and will prefer finding teachers who will say what their itching ears want to hear instead of truth (see 2 Timothy 4:3-5 above).

So, how do we, like Timothy, be intentional about staying alert? Paul's admonition to the Thessalonians sheds some light on this question. After using the labor pains analogy as a warning to stay alert, Paul contrasts the spiritually unprepared with sons and daughters of the light, who should be awake and alert, waiting for Christ's return.

> For you are all children of light, children of the day. We are not of the night or of the darkness. So then let us not sleep, as others do, but let us keep awake and be sober.
>
> —1 Thessalonians 5:5-6

Whether you are "of the night" or a "child of light" isn't dependent on what you call yourself, what doctrine you hold to, or what church you attend, but by what you do when the light of the Son shines into your life. Do you pull the covers over your head and go back to sleep? Or do you wake up and get moving? The people of the night will always reach for the covers while the children of light strap on their bullet-proof vests and helmets. We see this in Paul's final admonition of this passage.

But since we belong to the day, let us be sober [alert], having put on the breastplate of faith and love, and for a helmet the hope of salvation.

—1 Thessalonians 5:8

While strapping on armor may seem a little drastic, it's a reminder that we aren't just doing spiritual work but also going into a spiritual battle. It's not enough for a soldier to roll out of bed and walk out onto the battlefield. Serious soldiers who expect to survive the battle strap on their armor and stay alert.

PUTTING ON FAITH, HOPE, AND LOVE

Unlike Paul's "armor of God" passage in Ephesians 6:10-18, which covers the entire battle gear of a soldier, Paul's directive to the Thessalonian church mentions only two pieces—a breastplate of faith and love and a helmet of hope for salvation (1 Thessalonians 5:8). These pieces are particularly vital because the head and chest are the most vulnerable parts of the human body. Paul uses these examples of essential armor to illustrate that if we want to stay alert in the spiritual war of life, it is essential that each day we put on faith, hope, and love.

Through faith we believe in a God we can't see. Through faith in Jesus, we have peace with the Father. Through faith in God's Word, we trust and obey. The author of Hebrews affirms that we can't draw near to God without a growing faith in him.

And without faith it is impossible to please him, for whoever would draw near to God must believe that he exists and that he rewards those who seek him.

—Hebrews 11:6

Genuine faith will always lead us to a hope that God will one day right all wrongs and invite us into his eternal kingdom. It's this kind of hope that allows us to endure the "inconvenient" afflictions that are a part of fulfilling our ministries. The very trials that Satan uses to snuff out our faith are the tools God uses to grow our hope in him.

The Holy Spirit who now abides in us is the reason for this hope. And through his presence in our lives, we can love the Lord our God with all our heart, soul, and mind and our neighbor as ourselves (Matthew 22:37-40). Putting on faith, hope, and love is how we stay alert and fulfill our ministry even when others are slipping into complacency and heresy.

REFLECT AND APPLY

What are some of the messages coming today from the church that are itching ears, drawing people away from the truth of God's Word, and lulling them to sleep?

CHAPTER THIRTY
LEANING INTO MESSINESS

For the time is coming when people will not endure sound teaching, but having itching ears they will accumulate for themselves teachers to suit their own passions, and will turn away from listening to the truth and wander off into myths. As for you, always be sober-minded, endure suffering, do the work of an evangelist, fulfill your ministry.

—2 Timothy 4:3-5

Bear one another's burdens, and so fulfill the law of Christ.

—Galatians 6:2

IN CHAPTER NINETEEN, WE LOOKED AT different kinds of suffering we can expect to face as we serve God. In this chapter, we will examine one more kind of suffering. This one doesn't come from the world but from those we serve in our own faith communities. One might think serving others who are also serving Christ would be easy. But sometimes the hardest people to love are those with whom we worship and share the Lord's Supper. This is typically because our expectations for those people are higher. But even if we are doing all God asks us to do, and sometimes especially when we are doing all God asks of us, there will be those who don't respond positively to our ministry.

FAITHFUL MINISTRY IS COSTLY

Paul warned Timothy that a time would come when the church he was pastoring would turn away from his teachings and run after false teachers (2 Timothy 4:3-4). Paul's answer to this is the second item on the ministry fulfillment checklist he gave Timothy: endure hardship, or suffering, without wavering from the ministry to which God had called him (2 Timothy 4:5).

Only by leaning into the messiness would Timothy be able to fulfill his calling. Giving of ourselves in genuine community is a beautiful experience, but it is also very costly. It has rightly been said that "there is no such thing as a faithful ministry that is not costly. A painless ministry is a shallow and fruitless ministry."[1]

LEARNING TO SERVE IN COMMUNITY

Before ministering cross-culturally in Africa, I didn't fully understand what it meant to live and serve in true community. This was because my pre-mission's life was very segmented. Each week I had work, personal time, and ministry responsibilities. Each segment of my life had its place, and rarely did the people, locations, or times overlap with each other.

Then I moved to a village in Tanzania, East Africa, where my education on living and ministering in community began. One big learning moment was the result of my failure to get those I was discipling to meet with me in any consistent way. I would remind them throughout the week of our discipleship meetings, prepare the Bible study, and wait for them to arrive. Week after week, I did more waiting than studying the Bible with these men as they rarely showed up.

Later, I realized this had less to do with their desire to study the Bible than our differing views of time and how we structured our days. Regardless of the reasons, it was evident that traditional discipleship training methods focused on meeting at a particular time to go through a predetermined curriculum would not work in my new setting. This initial failure proved a blessing in disguise as through it God showed me a better way to do discipleship.

The people in this village were farmers. They ate what they planted and also grew cash crops like rice, cashews, and sesame to help themselves through the lean months. Subsistence farming is a serious matter, as one's very life depends on the harvest brought in each year. A bad year can reduce a family to poverty while a couple bad years can mean life or death to vulnerable family members. Because of all that is dependent on a harvest, the villagers were afraid to try new methods of farming, even if these held the promise of being more sustainable and profitable.

One way we were able to serve the community was through a demonstration farm where we could plant different crops side by side and learn together what farming practices worked best without risk to personal harvests. Farming a five-acre property by hand meant hiring a number of men from our church to help with ongoing maintenance. For months we worked side by side, digging, slashing, and preparing the land. We quickly found a rhythm to our days, which included praying each morning before work and sharing meals of sweet potatoes and sweeter tea during breaks. Before I knew it, we were also talking about what the Bible had to say about matters of faith, family, and church. At some point without my realizing it, discipleship had started to happen.

Why? Because we were now doing life together and these moments were happening organically instead of being regulated to an official time, place, and program. As these discipleship moments became the norm day in and day out, I realized that ministry was more than something I went and did at an appointed time but rather something I lived in a shared community.

Maintaining Community is Costly

Another important lesson I learned from this experience was that creating and maintaining a loving community is a lot harder than creating and maintaining a demonstration farm. While we had beautiful times of prayer and fellowship, there were also situations that stretched my capacity to live in unity with these same men. One particularly hurtful time resulted when a worker ignored theft and property damages on the farm because he'd become disgruntled with his pay. It felt like a personal betrayal. It took time, grace, and another brother mediating between us to restore our friendship. It wasn't a pretty situation, but it became an example to us and others in the community of how the love of Christ can bring healing to a broken relationship.

Living out the gospel in our families, churches, and neighborhoods will often mean enduring personal sacrifices and hardships for the glory of God and the good of the community. Galatians 6:2 instructs, "Bear one another's burdens, and so fulfill the law of Christ." What law is the law of Christ? It is what Jesus himself called the greatest commandments: love the Lord our God with all our heart, soul, and mind, and love our neighbor as our self (Matthew 22:37-40). It is this law that Jesus ultimately fulfilled on the cross.

Fulfilling our ministry and fulfilling the law of Christ go hand-in-hand. Loving the same broken people day in and day out can get messy and very inconvenient. At times, this will be a burden we suffer under as we serve God. But this burden becomes lighter when we keep in mind that this is how the gospel breaks into lives and transforms entire communities. This is why we must lean into the "inconveniences" of others instead of hiding behind walls or running off to engage in easier segments of our life.

Of course we do need to take time as Jesus did to get away with God and our loved ones (Mark 6:31; Luke 5:15-16). Creating healthy boundaries allows us to live and minister sustainably. Unfortunately, in many of our ministries we aren't occasionally stepping **out** of a genuine community to regroup but occasionally stepping *into* a genuine community to engage. Our ministry will never fully be fulfilled until we reverse this mindset.

REFLECT AND APPLY

When have you experienced genuine community? How can this impact your ministry going forward?

CHAPTER THIRTY-ONE
TWO SIDES OF PROCLAMATION

For the time is coming when people will not endure sound teaching, but having itching ears they will accumulate for themselves teachers to suit their own passions, and will turn away from listening to the truth and wander off into myths. As for you, always be sober-minded, endure suffering, do the work of an evangelist, fulfill your ministry.

—2 Timothy 4:3-5

But how can they call on him they have not believed in? And how can they believe without hearing about him? And how can they hear without a preacher? And how can they preach unless they are sent?

—Romans 10:14-25b

THE THIRD ITEM ON PAUL'S MINISTRY FULFILLMENT checklist for Timothy was doing "the work of an evangelist." The word evangelism can create a negative reaction when it conjures up images of high-pressure salespeople pushing the Good News on others. When I was a child, my family sat through a time-share sales pitch. The deal was that if you listened to a thirty-minute promotion, you would get free admission to an amusement park regardless of your final decision. After listening politely, my parents said no to the timeshare. This sent the salesman into an even more frenzied pitch, all while dangling the park tickets just out of reach.

The worst part was that the office we were in was right outside the park, so laughter and screams from children having the time of their lives could be heard throughout the presentation. These salespeople were clever but ignorant of how my dad would react in this situation. After persevering through forty-five minutes of haranguing, he stormed out of the presentation and up to the front desk, where he demanded our tickets. Seeing the look in his eyes, they promptly handed them over.

HIGH PRESSURE EVANGELISM

As I reflect on that incident, I can see how many people approach evangelism in the same way this time-share salesman approached his job. Load on the pressure, dangle the free "entry ticket" just out of reach, and try to close the deal. It's no wonder unbelievers get frustrated and walk away.

That isn't what Jesus meant when he said to go into all the world and make disciples (Matthew 28:19).

If we love Jesus and are living in community, telling others about him will flow naturally from us without props, pressure, or a sales pitch. If we have a spring of living water in us (John 4:14), it will bubble over naturally into our interactions with others. Sharing Christ should be the normal outflow of every believer who genuinely loves God with all their heart, soul, and mind.

That said, there is a specific role in the church for people who are particularly gifted in the area of evangelism. One list Paul gives of spiritual giftings includes evangelists along with apostles, prophets, shepherds, and teachers (Ephesians 4:11). So when Paul tells Timothy to "do the work of an evangelist," he could be expecting Timothy to fulfill the office of an evangelist or simply encouraging Timothy to see proclaiming the gospel as an integral part of his general ministry. Let's focus on the second option because it applies to every believer.

EVANGELIZING BELIEVERS AND THE LOST

Evangelism is often thought of as something focused on the lost. But we shouldn't neglect proclaiming the gospel to believers as well. As we've seen, even those who already believe are prone to wander into false teachings and sin. So it is integral that we constantly remind each other of gospel truths through diverse platforms like sermons, music, prayer, and above all, our own lives. As we proclaim God's Word to fellow believers, we must ensure that gospel truths are always at the core of our message. Instead of trying to be relevant to whatever is trending socially, let's be more concerned with exalting Christ. It's not about bringing something new to astound but bringing something old to remember.

The other side of proclamation is telling a lost world about Jesus. One need only look around this world to see that God has already proclaimed his presence through his creation. In his Commentary on Genesis, sixteen century reformer John Calvin wrote:

> The Creation is quite like a spacious and splendid house, provided and filled with the most exquisite and the most abundant furnishings. Everything in it tells us of God.
>
> —John Calvin[1]

Calvin's words echo King David's exclamation in Psalm 19:1: "The heavens declare the glory of God, and the sky above proclaims his handiwork." That said, God left it to his children to share the good news of how we can know God through his son, Jesus Christ. The apostle Paul reminds us of this responsibility in his letter to the Roman church.

> How then will they call on him [Christ] in whom they have not believed? And how are they to believe in him of whom they have never heard? And how are they to hear without someone preaching? And how are they to preach unless they are sent? As it is written, "How beautiful are the feet of those who preach the good news!"
>
> —Romans 10:14-15b

The obvious answer to these questions is that the lost can't believe if no one goes to tell them the good news of Christ. The bottom line is that if we want to share the hope of Christ with the lost in natural, impactful ways, we must live among them. Too often we see evangelism as something we do around certain events. As a part of these "evangelistic" events, we go to places we don't normally go, do things we don't normally do, talk to people we don't normally interact with, and say words we don't normally say.

Sadly, the only normal thing is that we usually get the same disappointing results. Good things can happen as a result of these one-off evangelism efforts. But they are often short-lived and lack the impact that comes from sharing Christ with others as we live alongside them.

Some dear friends of mine were struggling with the realization that they were spending too much of their lives in their local church building instead of with the lost. As a dynamic couple who stepped up whenever there was a need, they found themselves overly involved in different church ministries. They were feeling convicted to go deeper with co-workers who didn't know God, but they knew this wouldn't be possible unless they cut back on commitments inside the church building.

But the very thought of stepping back from church ministry was causing this couple to feel guilty. They asked for prayer that God would free them from these feelings of guilt and that they would spend regular time with the lost. May we all pray that God would save us from making his house the thing that keeps us from proclaiming his gospel to a lost world!

REFLECT AND APPLY

What does it look like or could it look like in your life to proclaim the gospel to both the believer and unbeliever?

CHAPTER THIRTY-TWO
COMPLETING OUR ASSIGNMENT

Preach the word; be prepared in season and out of season; correct, rebuke and encourage—with great patience and careful instruction. For the time will come when people will not put up with sound doctrine. Instead, to suit their own desires, they will gather around them a great number of teachers to say what their itching ears want to hear. They will turn their ears away from the truth and turn aside to myths. But you, keep your head in all situations, endure hardship, do the work of an evangelist, discharge all the duties of your ministry.

—2 Timothy 4:2-5 (NIV)

THE FINAL ITEM IN PAUL'S MINISTRY FULFILLMENT checklist for Timothy was to "fulfill your ministry" (2 Timothy 4:5). Or depending on the translation used, to fully discharge, carry out, and complete all the duties of his ministry assignment. As we read through Paul's two letters to Timothy, we see that Timothy was stationed at the church of Ephesus with some clear duties and expectations.

Chief among these was putting down false teachings while bringing the church back to the gospel of Jesus Christ (1 Timothy 1:3-4; 2 Timothy 4:3-4). Along with this, Timothy was to serve the church by being a godly example (1 Timothy 4:12). He was to read the Scriptures publicly as well as preach and teach the gospel (1 Timothy 4:12; 2 Timothy 4:2). He was also to use his gift of overseer to shepherd the congregation (1 Timothy 4:14; 2 Timothy 1:6).

In summary, his ministry was to rescue this church from heresy and shepherd them to a healthy place.

HOW WE FULFILL OUR MINISTRY

Paul was urging Timothy to "discharge all the duties" of his ministry (v. 5, NIV) because it's natural to want to walk away when times get hard. The Bible is filled with stories of God's people wanting to be released from their service before they'd fulfilled all he was asking them to do. Why? Because God often asked his servants to do things that went against their natural inclinations or were beyond what they felt they could accomplish in their own strength.

Serving God is not always about what we want to do or what comes naturally to us. It's about stepping out in faith and obedience and doing what God asks us to do. God chose Timothy to fulfill this ministry because he wanted to do specific things in and through Timothy. To walk away before God's appointed time would be to cut short all God had for both Timothy and those he was appointed to serve.

BEING RELEASED FROM A FULFILLED MINISTRY

Much has been written about being called into ministry. But I haven't found many resources on how to know when a ministry responsibility has been fulfilled and when we are free to move on. If we are walking in obedience to God, we will eventually fulfill our ministry, and it will come to an end. For many of us, this may happen multiple times over the course of our lives.

So it's important to look at what it means to end a fulfilled ministry in an intentional and Spirit-led way before moving on to serve God in a different capacity. Having the assurance that God has released you from your current ministry can be the difference between ending a ministry well and running away prematurely from your God-given assignment. For this reason, it's just as important to have a call that releases you from your ministry as it was to have a call that committed you to that ministry in the first place.

Too often these days, if someone declares that God called them to do something, people feel this can't be challenged. This comes from the false belief that our faith and callings are individualistic endeavors and that we can discern God's will for our lives in a vacuum. Because of this misconception, many people are doing ministries that don't fit their spiritual giftings or are doing things God never asked them to do.

Let me be clear that there's nothing wrong with sensing a personal call from God. There are scriptural precedents for God calling individuals in isolation (Abraham, Moses, Joshua, Gideon, to name a few). But these were typically miraculous events we find in the Old Testament. In the church era, both in the New Testament and early church practices, we see callings usually happening within a faith community.

Leaders of the church of Antioch prayerfully sensed the Holy Spirit's call on Paul and Barnabas to do mission work (Acts 13). Timothy's call to ministry came from Paul, his spiritual father, and was confirmed by the laying on of hands by elders (1 Timothy 4:14; 2 Timothy 1:6). When early church father St. Francis of Assisi felt a call towards preaching the gospel, he didn't trust his own spiritual perceptions but humbly sought the spiritual counsel of Sister Clare and Brother Silvester.[1]

These are just a few examples. When our personal callings are affirmed by our spiritual community, who are themselves under the guidance of the Holy Spirit, we can be confident our calling is from God. And if this is the model for being called into ministry, it should also be the model to be released from ministry.

My wife and I were clearly called to our last ministry location in the Middle East, which was affirmed by the eldership of our local church. Due in part to the global pandemic, we felt our time might be coming to an end. We wanted to be confident this was God releasing us and not just our own impression. So we borrowed a historic church practice from the Quaker tradition called a Clearness Committee.

The Quakers are a diverse Protestant denomination that was founded on the principle that every believer has the ability to experience the guiding light of Christ within them. Although this concept has been taken too far by many, I can appreciate the desire to hear the voice of God's Spirit over our own. A desire that is reflected in their worship times, which are often led by an attitude of expectant silence. They will sit in this "expectant silence" until the Holy Spirit moves in one of their members and gives them a word to share with the congregation. Only at that point will the silence be broken for the edification of the church body. This format is followed in an effort to weed out human thoughts from God's counsel. The clearness committee in which we participated was based on this same principle, but its usual focus is to seek individual guidance for vocations, marriages, social issues, and ministry callings.[2]

HOW TO HAVE A CLEARNESS COMMITTEE

The following practices are among those my wife and I and many others have found helpful in forming their own clearness committee.[3]

- Begin by bathing the process in prayer and fasting just as the Antioch church was doing when the Holy Spirit commissioned Paul and Barnabas (Acts 13:2-3).

- Invite five to ten spiritual leaders and discerning friends as participants. The invitation should explain what a clearness committee is and on what you are seeking discernment. Be detailed.

- Ask someone with spiritual discernment to emcee the event. This will free you from the burden of trying to lead and allow you to be fully present in this emotional event.

- Gather the clearness committee members all together in one place.

- The emcee should invite the Holy Spirit to come and guide this time, then give you the opportunity to briefly summarize what you shared in your invitation. It is also important to affirm that you are submitting yourself to this group's authority and the authority of the Holy Spirit.

- Set parameters in advance that the committee should ask clarifying open-ended questions only. The emcee should redirect if people begin offering advice or solutions instead. This time should be about listening to the Holy Spirit rather than solving a problem.

- For the next step, the emcee should invite each committee member to pray out loud for guidance on the situation.

- Committee members should then sit before the Lord in silence, waiting to hear any words of insight or guidance he may give. This may be a verse, image, impression of a word, or thought. While this can seem uncomfortable and last a while, don't rush the Spirit. If someone receives a word, they should share it with the group, who will then "test the spirits" (1 John 4: 1) through scriptural truth and unity in the Holy Spirit. By this point, a theme will often begin appearing among the participants.

- Once all have given their input, the emcee should create a summary statement that includes any clarity gained during this time.

- The emcee can then bring the meeting to a close by inviting everyone to a time of giving thanks to God for his presence and guidance.

CONFIDENCE AND COMMITMENT

Sometimes clearness regarding the situation on which you are seeking guidance will emerge from just one meeting. Other times, it may take a series of meetings. This isn't a reflection of your faith but the journey on which God is taking you. The time with your clearness committee also may or may not affirm what you were personally sensing.

Regardless of what word you receive from your committee, there is a confidence that this response is from a community that is united in the Holy Spirit. Having placed yourself under this committee's authority, keep in mind that you are now obligated to obey any guidance the Holy Spirit has given to you through this time.

REFLECT AND APPLY

How would moving into a new ministry be different if you had a clear release from your previous assignment?

Going Deeper

Suggested Activities

1. Read a book or watch a movie in which the theme is on Christ's return. Don't get hung up on eschatological details but rather dwell on the reality of Christ's imminent return and our need to be about is business.

2. If you aren't already part of a small group of believers, make time in your schedule to join one. Commit to being vulnerable and going deep on multiple levels with this community.

3. Do an act of kindness towards your literal neighbor. Use this opportunity to introduce yourself if you haven't already.

4. Create a map of your block/street, indicating who lives in each house and a brief description of them. Hang this map in a place where you will see it and be reminded to pray for your neighbors and interact with them. Look expectantly for God to open up opportunities to listen and serve your neighbors.

Suggested Reading:

Organic Church: Growing Faith Where Life Happens by Cornelius Cole

The Art of Neighboring by Jay Pathak & Dave Runyon

SECTION NINE:
LEAVING A LASTING LEGACY

Lord and Master, Jesus Christ, Co-eternal Word of the Father, to save us, you became like us in every way, except without sin. Move us not only to be hearers of the Word but also doers, and to bring forth good fruit, thirty, sixty, or a hundred times what was sown and be received into the kingdom of heaven. Let your love overtake our hearts, for the gospel proclaims you, O Savior and Guardian of our souls and bodies, and to you we ascribe all glory.

—Liturgy of St. Mark
Fourth Century Liturgy, Orthodox Church of Alexandria

CHAPTER THIRTY-THREE
BUILDING A LEGACY THROUGH INTEGRITY

For I am already being poured out as a drink offering, and the time of my departure has come. I have fought the good fight, I have finished the race, I have kept the faith. Henceforth there is laid up for me the crown of righteousness, which the Lord, the righteous judge, will award to me on that day, and not only to me but also to all who have loved his appearing.

—2 Timothy 4:6-8

FINAL GOODBYES ARE HARD. SO MUCH SO that I'm always tempted to rush through them or avoid them altogether. But when I think of how Paul used his farewell to the Ephesian elders to reinforce his ministry legacy, I recognize that skipping good-byes would result in missing out on potentially impactful moments. If God allows us the opportunity for an intentional farewell at the end of our ministries or lives, we'd do well to take advantage of that.

But we don't always know in advance when such opportunities will come, so we aren't always prepared. While less than ideal, this doesn't ruin our chances of leaving behind lasting legacies. The reality is that we don't create legacies in our last moments with others. We only reinforce the ones we've already made. Living our lives now in a way that allows us to give our farewell speeches with integrity is far more important than whether we actually get the chance to give them.

In Paul's own farewell speech to Timothy (see focus passage above), it is clear that Paul understood this truth. He uses the imagery of "finishing the race" to declare that he has faithfully completed all God asked of him. He has kept the faith. Because of this, he can look forward to receiving his victor's crown from Jesus.

This isn't the first time Paul used this "finishing the race" imagery. We saw him use it before in his farewell speech to the Ephesian church elders.

But I do not account my life of any value nor as precious to myself, if only
I may finish my course and the ministry that I received from the Lord
Jesus.

—Acts 20:24

In both farewell speeches, Paul connects the imagery of finishing a race
with having a full and completed ministry, but only to the Ephesian elders
does he add specific details of what this looks like. In this farewell address,
we can see four principles that if followed will help us finish our ministries
with intentionality and a Christ-honoring legacy. We will examine one of
these principles in each of the remaining chapters.

- Legacy principle #1: Our lives will either support or undermine our
  message (Acts 20:17-20).

- Legacy principle #2: Staying on course means being sensitive to the
  Holy Spirit's direction (Acts 20:22-24).

- Legacy principle #3: Lasting legacies are built intentionally and with
  departure in mind (Acts 20:25-35).

- Legacy principle #4: At its core, serving Christ's church is about caring
  and connecting (Acts 20:36-38).

Paul started off his farewell speech to the Ephesian elders by reminding
them of the core gospel message he'd taught while among them of
"repentance toward God and of faith in our Lord Jesus Christ" (Acts 20:21).
As already noted, Paul is spotlighting the true gospel because he knows that
false teachers with a counterfeit message will eventually try to creep into the
Ephesian church. It is worth noting that of all the things he could have said

to validate his gospel as the true one, he simply reminded them that he was a man of integrity.

> You yourselves know how I lived among you the whole time from the first day that I set foot in Asia, serving the Lord with all humility and with tears and with trials that happened to me through the plots of the Jews; how I did not shrink from declaring to you anything that was profitable, and teaching you in public and from house to house.
>
> —Acts 20: 18-20

OUR LIVES WILL EITHER SUPPORT OR UNDERMINE OUR MESSAGE

Paul understood that people's lives either support or undermine the messages they bring. By pointing out the honorable way he lived among them, he added credibility to the gospel he had preached. By contrast, he was also bringing to their attention how false teachers undermine their own message through their ungodly lifestyle. This principle is rooted in the teachings of Jesus in his Sermon on the Mount.

> Beware of false prophets, who come to you in sheep's clothing but inwardly are ravenous wolves. You will recognize them by their fruits. Are grapes gathered from thornbushes? . . . Thus you will recognize them by their fruits.
>
> —Matthew 7:15-16, 20

Jesus compared false prophets to ravenous wolves in sheep's clothing. By drawing attention to their deceptive disguise, he highlighted that it's hard to perceive the true nature of a prophet or preacher by what they say. On the surface, their messages are usually sprinkled with just enough truth to camouflage the lies.

To help us distinguish a genuine prophet from a false one, Jesus gave us a tool in the form of a question: "Are grapes gathered from thornbushes?"

The answer may seem obvious, but his audience would have known from experience that the berries of a Palestinian buckthorn bush can look like grapes upon a casual glance.[1] That said, if you were to eat the berries, the resulting cramping and diarrhea would quickly expose their true identity. With this question, Jesus was equating the poisonous qualities of these thornbush berries with the deceptive messages of false prophets. What at first glance may seem a refreshing word from God can end up being a destructive false teaching once we take the time to inspect the fruit it bears in the life of the messenger. If the fruit is toxic, it will result in spiritual cramping and diarrhea. Then we will know it is a false word.

In Ephesians 5:1-18, Paul gives us an entire list of the different toxic fruits false messengers bear. These include sexually immorality, greed, and crude, uncontrolled speech. No matter how charismatic a ministry leader may be, if they are bearing these fruits in their lives, the Bible tells us to reject their message and distance ourselves from them because they are under God's wrath.

> Let no one deceive you with empty words, for because of these things [toxic fruits] the wrath of God comes upon the sons of disobedience. Therefore do not become partners with them, for at one time you were darkness, but now you are light in the Lord. Walk as children of light.
>
> —Ephesians 5:6-8

This strong warning reminds us that we cannot live in darkness preaching the light. When those to whom we minister inspect our lives, there should be nothing that contradicts the gospel message we bring.

277

In Paul's farewell speech to the elders of Ephesus, he purposely puts an interrogation light on his own life to demonstrate that they can believe the gospel he brought, reminding them, "For three years I did not cease night and day to admonish everyone with tears" (Acts 20:31).

If Paul wasn't the man he claimed to be, the elders would have known it instantly. When you live your life deep in community for that long, the real you is bound to come out. To be certain, Paul wasn't perfect the entire time he was with them. That isn't what he was getting at. His point was that he consistently modeled the truths of the gospel by serving them in humility and love.

This is what God desires from his messengers of the gospel. He is not expecting perfection but that we be people of integrity. He knows spiritual perfectionism is a double-edged sword with the name legalism etched on its blade. We will fall on this sword if we try to be the spiritual leader who has it all together spiritually. In doing this, we will simply portray an image that isn't true and set a standard people can't copy. We will be failures twice over because of our pride.

But if we live out the gospel humbly as imperfect people, then what we preach with our lives will support what we preach in our ministries. This will be the legacy we leave when we are no longer physically present to proclaim the gospel.

REFLECT AND APPLY

In what ways does your personal life support the gospel you preach? In what ways is your personal life undermining the gospel you preach?

CHAPTER THIRTY-FOUR
BUILDING A LEGACY THROUGH DEPENDENCY

For I am already being poured out as a drink offering, and the time of my departure has come. I have fought the good fight, I have finished the race, I have kept the faith. Henceforth there is laid up for me the crown of righteousness, which the Lord, the righteous judge, will award to me on that day, and not only to me but also to all who have loved his appearing.

—2 Timothy 4:6-8

THROUGHOUT THE BOOK OF ACTS, PAUL'S general ministry plan was to go to prominent cities across the Roman Empire, where he would proclaim the gospel message, then gather a church together with those who believed. As communities were transformed by the gospel, the religious and political leaders felt threatened and would respond with persecution. This usually prompted Paul to move on to the next strategic city, where he would once again proclaim the gospel and start a church.

But though Paul had a strategy that guided his ministry, he was alert to any changes the Holy Spirit wanted to make along the way. We see this in Paul's farewell speech to the Ephesian elders when he set aside his normal ministry strategy to travel to Jerusalem.

> And now, behold, I am going to Jerusalem, constrained by the Spirit, not knowing what will happen to me there, except that the Holy Spirit testifies to me in every city that imprisonment and afflictions await me. But I do not account my life of any value nor as precious to myself, if only I may finish my course and the ministry that I received from the Lord Jesus, to testify to the gospel of the grace of God.
>
> —Acts 20:22-24

If you were a prophet or teacher from God, Jerusalem was probably the last place on earth you would want to go. This is ironic since it was and still is Israel's center of worship to God. On one trip to Jerusalem, Jesus said of this city:

> O Jerusalem, Jerusalem, the city that kills the prophets and stones those who are sent to it!
>
> —Luke 13:34

Paul knew his trip to Jerusalem would end in "imprisonment and afflictions," but he still went because he was "constrained by the Holy Spirit" to do so. He was willing to sacrifice his life to stay the course and finish the ministry he'd received from God. This leads us to our second legacy principle.

STAYING ON COURSE MEANS BEING SENSITIVE TO THE HOLY SPIRIT'S DIRECTION

Another example of Paul yielding to the Holy Spirit over his own ministry strategy was on his second missionary journey. Heading north from his sending church in Antioch to the eastern corner of the Mediterranean Sea, he then turned west, probably following the Roman road, called the Via Sebastes (Acts 16:1-5). Had he continued westward on this route, he would have ended up in Asia Minor. Since his modus operandi had been to go to prominent cities of the Roman Empire, it would make sense that he would have ended up in Ephesus, capital of that region. But the Holy Spirit had other plans.

> And they went through the region of Phrygia and Galatia, having been forbidden by the Holy Spirit to speak the word in Asia. And when they had come up to Mysia, they attempted to go into Bithynia, but the Spirit

of Jesus did not allow them. So, passing by Mysia, they went down to Troas. And a vision appeared to Paul in the night: a man of Macedonia was standing there, urging him and saying, "Come over to Macedonia and help us." And when Paul had seen the vision, immediately we sought to go on into Macedonia, concluding that God had called us to preach the gospel to them.

—Acts 16:6-10

The cities where the Holy Spirit prevented them from preaching were all in Asia Minor. Troas was a port city on the Aegean Sea four hundred miles westward. More importantly for Paul, it was where he finally received clear directions for the next step of his journey through a vision from the Holy Spirit.

This series of events demonstrates that while it is wise to have a ministry strategy, it is also important that our strategy doesn't replace our dependence on the Holy Spirit. In Paul's travels, he'd have had to bypass many cities in need of the gospel. It was crucial that he be aware of the Holy Spirit's guidance and obey it over his own intuition or plans.

It was also important that Paul not get ahead of the Holy Spirit and assume he knew God's long-term plan. At every fork in the road, God gave Paul just enough information to get him to his next decision point. It wasn't until Troas that God's ultimate plan was revealed. He wanted Paul to take the gospel to the European continent, which had yet to receive the gospel. Had Paul not been sensitive to the voice of the Holy Spirit and instead forged ahead with ministry as usual, he'd have missed the opportunity to bring the good news of Christ to a new part of the world that would prove fertile ground for God's kingdom.

God's guidance will not always follow our well-planned strategies. Sometimes it will even fly in the face of "fruitful practice" principles. This is when like Paul we must "count our lives as nothing" (Acts 20:24) if we want to complete the course God has set out for us. At many junctures in our lives, God will ask us to take turns that make little sense to us and that also demand we sacrifice our own plans and desires. Sometimes we get to see the reasons behind God's directives. More often, we just have to be content to faithfully obey, trusting that God will use our obedience to accomplish his plans.

STAYING ALERT TO THE HOLY SPIRIT'S DIRECTIONS

In this race called life, there is no such thing as an obviously laid-out course. We are usually running full speed ahead, tired and feeling out of our element, when we are required to make decisions that set new trajectories for our lives and ministry. If we aren't running in step with the Holy Spirit, it's natural to choose the path of least resistance or get paralyzed by indecision. In these situations, we often look for heavenly signs that easily mark our way. We want the ease of impersonal road signs when God's desire is to communicate his directions to us in the context of a relationship.

As Paul ran his race in tandem with the Holy Spirit, there were very clear ways God communicated his directives. Below I include a list of incidents in Paul's life that are representative of different ways we see the Holy Spirit communicating his will to believers throughout Scripture. Examining how the Holy Spirit communicated to Paul can help us be alert and ready to recognize God's directions when he communicates them to us.

- Audible voice (Acts 9:4-6).

- Divine connections with people (Acts 9:10-19).

- Unity in faith community (Acts 13:1-4).

- Actions of others or life circumstances that we can't control (Acts 13:50-52, 25:12).

- Visions, dreams, trances (Acts 16:6-10, 18:9-11, 22:17-18).

- Strong impression or conviction (Acts 20:22).

- Prophetic words from others (Acts 21:10).

- Visit from Jesus (Acts 23:11).

- Visit from an angel (Acts 23:11).

- Instructions in Scripture (2 Timothy 3:16; Psalm 119:105).

REFLECT AND APPLY

Think of a time in your life when you needed to make a major decision. What process did you use to make that decision? Did the Holy Spirit direct you in any of the ways above?

CHAPTER THIRTY-FIVE
BUILDING A LEGACY THROUGH INTENTIONALITY

I have fought the good fight, I have finished the race, I have kept the faith.

—*2 Timothy 4:7*

PAUL CONTINUES HIS FAREWELL ADDRESS TO THE Ephesian elders by laying out how he'd purposefully ministered to the church of Ephesus in a manner that would help them succeed without him. Because he'd known he wouldn't be with them forever, he'd intentionally encouraged their spiritual maturity and interdependence on each other. From the passage (Acts 20:18-35), we get the impression that these things didn't just happen naturally, but that Paul implemented them from the beginning and with his imminent departure in mind.

Specifically, we see in his farewell address three areas by which Paul had set up the Ephesian church for success after he left. These three areas were teaching them the whole Word of God, appointing and empowering leadership, and modeling what it meant to work hard and live generously in community. These same areas should be at the center of ministry for any spiritual leader who desires to leave a lasting legacy. Which brings us to our third legacy principle.

LASTING LEGACIES ARE BUILT INTENTIONALLY AND WITH DEPARTURE IN MIND

Why do people in court swear to tell the truth, the whole truth, and nothing but the truth? Because by holding back or adding to the truth, we can manipulate it to fit our own agenda. That's what false teachers and cults do. They over-focus on those parts of the Bible that fit their agenda and ignore or dismiss the rest. Here are some examples.

- Jesus was a good teacher, but he never claimed to be God.

- The New Testament's message is for the modern-day believer, but the Old Testament is outdated and irrelevant.

- God is love, so he accepts all people the way they are.

Each of these statements has an element of God's truth in them. But they do not contain his whole truth. And if you sniff them up close, they smell like smoke straight from the pit of hell.

TEACH THE WHOLE WORD OF GOD

This is why Paul was so adamant when addressing the first area in which he'd purposefully prepared the Ephesian church for his departure.

Therefore I testify to you this day that I am innocent of everyone's blood, for I did not shrink back from declaring to you the whole plan of God.

—Acts 20:26-27

Declaring himself innocent of everyone's blood might seem a dramatic statement even for Paul. But what he was stressing here was that if anyone in the Ephesian church ended up going to hell for rejecting Christ, their blood would not be on his hands (see Ezekiel 33) because he'd courageously and consistently taught them the whole gospel and nothing but the gospel. This in contrast to false teachers who cherry-picked from the gospel message to create their own appealing belief systems.

It isn't surprising that false teachers use this strategy. Dressing up a lie to look like the truth is a trick they have learned from their father Satan, who knows it's easier to swallow poison if mixed with a spoonful of honey. He demonstrated this in the Garden of Eden when he told Eve:

> You will not surely die. For God knows that when you eat of it your eyes will be opened . . .
>
> —Genesis 3:4b-5

While true, this was hardly the whole truth. While Adam and Eve didn't die physically at that moment, their actions opened up the doors of death and hell for all humanity. Satan later tried this same technique when he tried to tempt Jesus in the wilderness (Matthew 4:1-11). With each temptation, he quoted fragments of Scripture in an attempt to get Jesus to bypass the Father's plan. Instead of engaging in debate with Satan as Eve had done (Genesis 3:1-5), Jesus simply quoted back to Satan the whole Word of God.

One example is when Satan was trying to get Jesus to jump off the pinnacle of the temple and let God save him, quoting from Psalm 91: "It is written, 'He will command his angels concerning you.'"

Jesus responded to Satan's manipulation of Scripture by quoting in turn from Moses's farewell address to the Israelites in Deuteronomy 6:16: "It is also written, 'You shall not put the Lord your God to the test.'"

In defeating Satan's false teachings by proclaiming the full context of God's Word back to him, Jesus was modeling how we should approach the Scriptures. As we make disciples, we must model how to handle God's Word in its fullness by the way we study and teach it. This is best done by teaching through entire books of the Bible systematically. It isn't the only way to handle God's Word, but it should be a consistent practice in our lives as it forces us to engage the whole truth of Scripture.

When we study and teach passages within their larger context, it helps to guard against the natural tendency of reading our own agendas into Scripture. It also forces us to grapple with the more uncomfortable parts of the Bible we might naturally ignore. If we want to ensure that the whole gospel message continues to be proclaimed in our ministries long after we are gone, then we need to proclaim the Word, the whole Word, and nothing but the Word, so help us, God!

Appoint Leadership and Empower Them

Officially, there are approximately fifty dictators around the world right now.[1] But that number would go up drastically if we counted presidents who have overstayed their constitutional invitations to rule. Once people get into powerful positions, they often imagine they are indispensable. This often leads to them refusing to identify or empower upcoming leaders out of fear that those leaders will undermine their authority and perhaps displace them. For the "good of the people," such autocrats remain in office until they die. When that happens, one of two things usually follows. Either another powerful person steps into the vacuum, or there is infighting until someone emerges the victor.

We often shake our heads at self-delusional dictators yet look in awe to the larger-than-life spiritual people who run our churches. While they may be both gifted and godly, if they aren't purposefully raising up a new generation of leaders to replace them, they may have a bit of dictator's blood running in their veins. The reality is that we all do. Even in our little ministry kingdoms, we often fall victim to the big-man syndrome.

That is why it is important in every ministry to guard against this natural tendency by raising up new leaders and empowering them. If we don't do this, we are setting up our ministries and churches for a leadership vacuum when we leave. In these vacuums, faith communities, like nations, will often reinvent themselves or experience infighting and splits.

Paul knew that after he left, the Ephesian church would experience challenges from without and within. To have any chance at Christ-centered longevity, they would need to have leaders chosen by the Holy Spirit, built up in the whole Word of God, and who had seen a real-life example of what would be expected of them. This is why he followed his proclamation of having preached the whole of God's Word with strong counsel.

> Pay careful attention to yourselves and to all the flock, in which the Holy Spirit has made you overseers, to care for the church of God, which he obtained with his own blood.
>
> —Acts 20:28

Under guidance of the Holy Spirit, Paul had purposefully chosen and empowered these leaders during his tenure in Ephesus (Acts 19), knowing that after his departure the Holy Spirit would complete what Paul had started through his ministry. It is important to note that although Paul had physically left Ephesus, he remained invested in the Ephesian believers' lives through his letters (including his epistle to the Ephesian church), prayers, visits, as well as appointing Timothy in his stead, all keys to the empowering process.

MODEL HEALTHY AND SUSTAINABLE PRACTICES

Paul was a hard worker, and it bothered him to see lazy people living off the misplaced generosity of the church. This was an offense he sternly addressed throughout his letters. In fact, he wrote to the Thessalonian church that we shouldn't even associate with parasites who take advantage of those trying to make an honest living and that any able-bodied person who refused to work shouldn't eat (2 Thessalonians 3:6-11).

While ministering to the church of Ephesus, Paul put aside his apostolic right to compensation and worked as a tentmaker so he could model what it meant to be a productive member of a community. In the final words of his farewell address, Paul reminded the Ephesian elders of his example.

> I coveted no one's silver or gold or apparel. You yourselves know that these hands ministered to my necessities and to those who were with me. In all things I have shown you that by working hard in this way we must help the weak and remember the words of the Lord Jesus, how he himself said, 'It is more blessed to give than to receive.'"
>
> —Acts 20:33-35

The law of Christ found in Galatians 6 gives us the model for a healthy community. This law says that each person should "bear his own load" in life (v.5) as much as they are able and not be a burden to others. Conversely, we are to help care for those unable to carry their burden for a time (v.2). People imitate what they see more than what they hear, so Paul made sure to model healthy and sustainable practices that he wanted to imbed into the church's culture.

In chapter twenty-six, I mentioned my time in Uganda, where I learned about biblical storytelling. This trip was also the first time I fully comprehended how important this modeling principle is. Every morning as my mentor and I started our long hike to the people we would be sharing stories with that day, we'd walk past his off-road motorcycle.

One day he explained that the reason we never used it for ministry was because we were modeling sustainable practices. If we rode that motorcycle to our ministry locations, future ministers would assume they couldn't do outreach ministry without a motorcycle. What might seem an insignificant matter was actually very important since it was beyond the ability of most local communities to afford one. Giving up our right to ride helped ensure that the ministry we were doing would live on after we were gone.

It takes humility and foresight to admit to ourselves that one day our ministries will end and those into whom we have invested our lives will go on without us. But whether we are able to admit it or not, it will happen. And whether we embrace this truth and intentionally do ministry with our departure in mind or put that thought off to another day will make the difference between our success or our failure.

REFLECT AND APPLY

Who are you (or who should you be) training up to take over your ministry after you are gone? How will you model sustainable practices?

CHAPTER THIRTY-SIX
BUILDING A LEGACY THROUGH CONNECTIVITY

I have fought the good fight, I have finished the race, I have kept the faith.

—*2 Timothy 4:7*

IF WE GO ABOUT OUR DUTIES WITH EXCELLENCE but don't love those to whom we minister in practical ways, we are wasting our time. Christ-like love requires more than just feelings. It requires tangible actions. In Paul's farewell speech to the Ephesian elders, we've seen how he cared for the church of Ephesus in many diverse and practical ways. These outpourings of Paul's love were conveyed in ways that connected with every part of their humanity.

As servants of God, we know it is our job to care for people's spiritual welfare. But humans are body, soul, and spirit. We need to connect with others on all these levels if we want to have a full and lasting impact on their lives. This brings us to our fourth and final legacy principle.

Serving Christ's Church Is About Caring and Connecting

When the apostle Paul finished his very important discourse to the Ephesian elders, he didn't just walk offstage and go about his business. This wasn't just a ministry event he'd successfully completed, which he could now disengage from to enjoy some personal time. What follows in the passage is a very personal and emotional description that demonstrates the depth of Paul's connection to these people spiritually, emotionally, and physically.

And when he had said these things, he knelt down and prayed with them all. And there was much weeping on the part of all; they embraced Paul and kissed him, being sorrowful most of all because of the word he had spoken, that they would not see his face again. And they accompanied him to the ship.

—Acts 20:36-38

CONNECTING WITH PEOPLE SPIRITUALLY

Paul's first action after delivering his speech was to kneel down and pray with the Ephesian elders. This was more than a quick benediction before rushing off to his waiting ship. He took time for a heartfelt prayer meeting.

Spending time lifting people up before God's throne is a wonderful way to care for them spiritually. But we can be of even greater encouragement when we spend time in-person with them in prayer. When people share the burdens of their lives with us, our natural response is to tell them we'll be praying for them. That's great if we remember to do it. But how much better to stop what we're doing and pray for them at that moment? It's a rare person who will decline such an offer.

These instant prayer moments also give us opportunities to follow up with those we've prayed with to see how God has been at work in their lives. These days, that may not even have to be in-person but by phone, Zoom, Facetime, or text-messaging. Praying in "real-time" with people may feel awkward, but it will become more comfortable with regular practice. This is just one of many ways to connect with people spiritually.

Connecting with People Emotionally

From the first day Paul arrived to serve at Ephesus until his last goodbye, he was shedding tears for and with this church (Acts 20:19, 31, 37). There was clearly a lot of genuine love between them, and from their emotional goodbye, it was obvious they would miss each other dearly. To connect this deeply with people, we need to be willing to invest in them emotionally. This may not come naturally to all of us, but it is an essential part of leaving a lasting legacy.

Whether this comes naturally to you or not, it would be beneficial to prayerfully reflect on Romans 12:9-21. This passage talks about genuine love being the mark of a true Christian, including many specific instructions on how to show that love practically.

> Let love be genuine . . . Love one another with brotherly affection. Outdo one another in showing honor . . . Contribute to the needs of the saints and seek to show hospitality . . . Rejoice with those who rejoice, weep with those who weep. Live in harmony with one another. Do not be haughty, but associate with the lowly . . . If possible, so far as it depends on you, live peaceably with all . . . Do not be overcome by evil, but overcome evil with good.
>
> —Romans 12:9-21

We see this kind of connection in emotionally healthy families where if one member is experiencing a major life event, the whole family walks through it with them. If it's the birth of a new baby, graduation, or wedding, they all rejoice together. If a death, loss of a job, or divorce, they all mourn together. When we see a person as "one of the family," we naturally want to invest in them emotionally. So it's important to make a conscious effort to see those to whom we minister as our spiritual family.

CONNECTING WITH PEOPLE PHYSICALLY

Paul didn't just pray and weep with the Ephesian elders as he made his farewells. The passage describes how they embraced and kissed each other, overcome with grief at saying goodbye. Then the elders insisted on physically escorting Paul to his ship to see him off (Acts 20:37-38).

Kissing other adults in greeting or farewell is not part of all our cultures today, but most of us are likely familiar with the biblical charge to "greet one another with a holy kiss." This actually comes in Paul's second epistle to the church of Corinth, where a kiss of greeting was indeed part of the culture just as it was for the Ephesians. In his closing words to the Corinthian believers, he challenges them to act like the family they are in Christ, calling them brothers and sisters.

> Finally, brothers and sisters, rejoice! Strive for full restoration, encourage one another, be of one mind, live in peace. And the God of love and peace will be with you. Greet one another with a holy kiss.
>
> —2 Corinthians 13:11-12, NIV

Paul's instructions as well as his example make clear that physically connecting with one another in family-appropriate ways is just as important to the church's collective health as the other more emotional and relational commands he gave them. Why? Because Paul knew we are both body and soul. If we are going to be a healthy church family, we need to be loving each other on both these levels.

That said, it is important as we display brotherly and sisterly love through physical touch, that we keep in mind the widely differing cultures and standards within the body of Christ on what is acceptable and appropriate. Let's be sensitive not to offend God or our brothers and sisters in moments of physical contact, but let's never forgo a crucial part of expressing love because of fear.

Another part of showing love physically is by being physically present in people's lives. When speaking to the Ephesian elders, Paul reminds them of how he interacted with them during his ministry "in public and from house to house" (Acts 20:20). Both of these are important and have their place when used properly. Large group meetings provide a venue for corporate celebrations, evangelism, and instruction. In contrast, small group gatherings allow the intimacy to connect more deeply into each other's lives.

These smaller gatherings go by many names, but they usually meet in homes or other natural community hubs and include some mix of worship, Scripture interaction, prayer, eating, and having fun together. As we share these experiences with each other, the beginnings of a true community form. It's impossible to be physically present in each other's lives if we are only connecting during the "greet your neighbor" moment in large group meetings. While potlucks and other similar events inside a church building can help build a general sense of community, they can never replace the intimacy of breaking bread with someone in their home.

I've had the privilege of being a part of a small group faith community. When done right, these people become your family. It doesn't take long before their lives begin to overlap with yours in many soul-enriching ways. Hosting gatherings and being physically present in people's lives at this level takes sacrifice and commitment. But it is a beautiful picture of true community.

REFLECT AND APPLY

Which of the three areas of connectivity (spiritually, emotionally, physically) is the most unnatural for you? What can you begin to do to grow in this area?

Going Deeper

Suggested Activities

1. Write out your farewell address using Paul's model in Acts 20, then commit to living in such a manner that you can someday deliver it with integrity to those you serve.

2. Make it a point this week to pray for people in "real time" (in-person) instead of just telling them you are praying for them. Then follow up with them to see how God is working in that situation.

3. Prayerfully ask God to bring you someone who can step into your ministry role when God calls you onwards or upwards, then begin to empower them to do just that.

Suggested Reading:

Seasons of a Leader's Life: Learning, Leading, and Leaving Your Legacy

by Jeff Iorg

Epilogue
Timothy's Legacy

Teach me to live that I may dread
The grave as little as my bed
Teach me to die that so I may
Rise glorious at that awesome day

—Thomas Ken
English Bishop and great hymn-writer of the 17 th century

Church tradition records that when Timothy was an old man, he was martyred on the streets of Ephesus during a festival held in honor of Dionysus, the Greek god of drunken orgies. Because this celebration had evolved into a night of unrestrained revelry and murder, Timothy, now bishop of this city, took it upon himself to fearlessly confront these cultists. With a strong voice, he called out to them to stop their madness and turn from worshipping idols. Instead of stopping, they turned their bloodlust on Timothy, showering him with stones and beating him with clubs until his body grew still.[1]

We honor the courageous martyrdom of this spiritual leader and minister who died like the fiery prophets of old. And we rejoice that although these pagans silenced his voice, his spiritual legacy lives on. Timothy's life and death bear witness that in every generation God can take a person plagued by fear and transform them into a mighty servant of God set ablaze with the Spirit of power, love, and a sound mind.

This same Spirit is available to all believers who desire like Timothy to fan the flame of their life and ministry. But it is only when we seek the Holy Spirit in his fullness that the flames of Pentecost transform us from flickering embers to a mighty fire set ablaze by God — a fire so full of passion for him that others will have to take notice and react, irresistibly drawn to or repelled by its intense light.

Dear reader, would that you also burn with this fire as you serve God with all your heart.

May "the grace of the Lord Jesus Christ and the love of God and the fellowship of the Holy Spirit be with you" (2 Corinthians 13:14).

FOOTNOTES AND SOURCES

CHAPTER 4

1. Eusebius (1965), *The History of the Church*, Williamson, G.A. transl., Harmonsworth: Penguin, p. 109.

CHAPTER 7

1. Warren, M. (n.d.). "Making Fire The Indian Way." Retrieved November 23, 2020, from http://medicinebow.net/media/articles-written-by-mark-warren/making-fire-the-indian-way/

2. "What Is The Sacred Fire?" (2020, July 30). Retrieved November 23, 2020, from https://danceforallpeople.com/about-fire/ page 112

CHAPTER 14

1. Macintyre, James. "Cracked: the Wesley Code." *The Independent*, Independent Digital News and Media, 23 Oct. 2011, https://www.independent.co.uk/news/uk/this-britain/cracked-the-wesley-code-909657.html

2. Wiersbe, W. (1988). Chapter 9, "Christians Courageous!" In 917411066 720942369 W. W. Wiersbe (Author), *Be Faithful*. Wheaton, IL: Victor Books

CHAPTER 15

1. Wignall, Nick. Why We Worry (and How to Stop), retrieved Dec 10, 2020 from https://nickwignall.com/why-we-worry/

CHAPTER 16

1. Timmons, J. (2018, January 05). "When Can a Fetus Hear: Womb Development Timeline." Retrieved January 07, 2020, from https://www.healthline.com/health/pregnancy/when-can-a-fetus-hear

2. Sweeton, J., Phys. D. (2017, November 15). "Change Your Brain With Cognitive Therapy." Retrieved January 22, 2020, from https://www.psychologytoday.com/intl/blog/workings-well-being/201711/change-your-brain-cognitive-therapy

3. Church Media Group, I. (n.d.). "Dr. Leaf 21 Day Brain Detox Program." Retrieved January 22, 2020, from https://21daybraindetox.com/

CHAPTER 17

1. Lunn-Rockliffe, D. (2011, February 17). History - Ancient History in Depth: "Christianity and the Roman Empire." Retrieved February 23, 2020, from https://silo.tips/download/christianity-and-the-roman-empire

2. Rasmussen, C. (2015, January 30). "The Ships of Ephesus - Part 2, Cargo Ship." Retrieved February 19, 2020, from https://holylandphotos.wordpress.com/2015/01/29/the-ships-of-ephesus-part-2-cargo-ship

CHAPTER 19

1. Munden, R. (2020, April 24). "Hello!" 2 Timothy Doc [E-mail to the author].

CHAPTER 21

1. T. (2020). Ancient Rome. Retrieved March 08, 2020, from https://www.ducksters.com/history/ancient_rome/housing_and_homes.php

2. Jasiński, J. (2018, October 28). "Chamber Pots in Ancient Rome." Retrieved March 10, 2020, from https://www.imperiumromanum.edu.pl/en/.../chamber-pots-in-ancient-rome/

3. W. (Director). (2016, December 01). "Chamber Pot: Portable Toilets through History" [Video file]. Retrieved March 10, 2020, from https://youtu.be/9qWWlUwFuJE

CHAPTER 23

1. Piper, John. Let Us Walk by the Spirit (March 1, 1981), Retrieved December 6, 2021, from https://www.desiringgod.org/messages/let-us-walk-by-the-spirit

CHAPTER 24

1. Piper, J. (2020). "A Solid Foundation," *Corona Virus and Christ* (p. 24). Wheaton, IL: Crosswalk

CHAPTER 25

1. Voice of Zion. "Introduction to Small Catechism." *LLC*, Sept. 2017, https://www.llchurch.org/post/introduction-to-the-small-catechism

2. T. (Director). (2017, May 25). "Orality Project" [Video file]. Retrieved April 05, 2020, from https://www.youtube.com/watch?v=gA1y4TWJIWY

CHAPTER 26

1. Young, T. (Writer). (2014, February 14). Number 13, "More Precious Than Gold" [Radio series episode]. The History of the Early Church Podcast.

2. Tyson, J. R. (2017). *The Great Athenasius, An Introduction to His Life and Work.* Cascade Books.

CHAPTER 30

1. Maclaren, A. (2019). 2 Timothy 4:5-6 Commentary. Retrieved May 08, 2020, from https://www.preceptaustin.org/2_timothy_45-13

CHAPTER 31

1. Calvin, John. *Commentary on Genesis, Volume 1.* (Christian Classics Ethereal Library, 1.1 edition, 2009), Page 84. Translated from the Original Latin by the Rev. John King, M.A.

CHAPTER 32

1. Brother Ugolino di Monte Santa Maria, *The Little Flowers of St. Francis* (Garden City, NY: Doubleday, 1958) pp. 74-48

2. Foster, R. J. (2018). "The Corporate Disciplines," *Celebration of Discipline: The path to Spiritual Growth* (pp. 180-183). San Francisco: HarperOne

3. Q. (Director). (2016, October 13). "How to Have a Quaker Clearness Committee" [Video file]. Retrieved May 11, 2020, from https://www.youtube.com/watch?v=kvNO4-leFOg

CHAPTER 33

1. Legionnaire, T. (2020). "False Prophets and Their Fruits." Retrieved June 05, 2020, from https://www.ligonier.org/learn/devotionals/false-prophets-and-their-fruits/

CHAPTER 35

1. P. (2020). "Current Dictators - List of Dictators In 2020." Retrieved June 18, 2020, from https://planetrulers.com/current-dictators/

EPILOGUE

1. "Acts of Timothy." (2019, October 28). Retrieved September 08, 2020, from https://en.wikipedia.org/wiki/Acts_of_Timothy, Usener, H. (n.d.). Timothy's Martyrdom Text. In 919598593 722288509 Lawson (Ed.), *Acts of Timothy* (pp. 48-51).

www.ingramcontent.com/pod-product-compliance
Lightning Source LLC
LaVergne TN
LVHW052014080426
835513LV00018B/2033